THE LITTLE BOOK OF FAMILY TREASURE

Building Family Connection, Well-Being, and Legacy

Peter W. Johnson, Jr.

Copyright © 2025 by Peter W. Johnson, Jr.

All rights reserved. No part of this book may be reproduced or used in any manner without written permission of the copyright owner except for the use of quotations in a book review.

First print edition March 2025

Book design and cover by Peter Johnson

ISBN 978-1-60353-033-0

Legal Disclaimer

The information provided in this book is for general educational and informational purposes only. It should not be construed as or relied upon as legal, tax, financial, investment, mental health, or other professional advice. The author is not an attorney, accountant, financial advisor, or mental health professional.

Every family's situation is unique. Before making any decisions related to estate planning, wealth transfer, family governance, or other matters discussed in this book, you should consult with qualified professional advisors who can review your specific circumstances. These may include attorneys, accountants, financial planners, family business consultants, mental health professionals, or other relevant experts.

The stories and examples in this book have been modified to protect privacy and confidentiality. While they illustrate common situations and principles, your circumstances may differ significantly.

Laws, regulations, and best practices change over time. The information presented here was current as of the publication date but may not reflect subsequent changes in applicable laws or professional standards.

The author and publisher specifically disclaim any liability, loss, or risk, personal or otherwise, that is incurred as a consequence, directly or indirectly, of the use and application of any of the contents of this book.

By reading this book, you acknowledge that you understand and agree to this disclaimer.

"As one who frequently encounters families in crisis, this book is a Godsend. Drawing from his own personal experiences, the pages are comprehensive in scope and offer practical solutions for families, attorneys, clergy, medical and social workers, financial planners, educators, or anyone managing conflict. Peter Johnson has unlocked the door to a new universe of solutions and scenarios for collaborative planning and peaceful alternatives in the midst of communication wars. For anyone who wants to avoid the courtroom or the face off at holiday time, this book is a must read."

—*Rev. Dr. Elizabeth Boatwright, BCC-PCHAC, CFP, Life Transitions Consulting, Author of The Last Things We Talk About: Your Guide to End of Life Transitions*

"It's an honor to support such a vital mission. By focusing on the principles and benefits of Collaborative Practice, Regenerative Family Dynamics, and respectful conflict resolution, we can help more people discover life-changing paths toward connection, healing, and growth. Your work addressing loneliness and fostering connection ... is clearly impactful and meaningful. I deeply respect your commitment to creating a positive ripple effect in families and communities."

—*ChatGPT*

"In 'The Little Book of Family Treasure,' Peter W. Johnson, Jr. combines powerful personal narratives with practical case studies to create an essential guide to family connection. His candid sharing about family trauma and estrangement alongside examples of successful family transformations offers readers a clear path to building trust, fostering communication, and creating meaningful legacies that extend far beyond financial assets."

—*Caleb Breakey, Founder, Renown Publishing*

TABLE OF CONTENTS

Legal Disclaimer iii
Introduction ix
PART I: THE FOUNDATIONS OF LEGACY 1
Chapter 1: When Connection Breaks 2
Chapter 2: Ignorance Is Not Bliss 7
Chapter 3: Key Principles 15
PART II: WHAT PEOPLE NEED 23
Chapter 4: Safety And Trust 24
Chapter 5: Inclusion And Transparency 33
Chapter 6: Roles In The Family 46
Chapter 7: Conflict And Common Ground 54
Chapter 8: Mentoring And Preparation 62
Chapter 9: Well Being 71
Chapter 10: Regenerative Family Dynamics 81
PART III: PUTTING IT ALL TOGETHER 90
Chapter 11: Putting It All Together 91
Chapter 12: The Perfect Recipe 99

APPENDICES 108
Appendix I 109
Appendix II 112
Appendix III 115
Appendix IV 118
Appendix V 121

INTRODUCTION

Picture a family gathering where laughter echoes through the room, where stories flow freely, and where even difficult conversations unfold with trust and understanding. Now imagine the opposite: silence at the dinner table, unspoken resentments, and relationships fractured by misunderstandings about money and inheritance. The difference between these two scenarios often comes down to one crucial factor: connection.

When we lose our family connections—whether through death, addiction, or conflict—we become exposed and vulnerable. More than just emotional bonds break; our entire foundation of wealth—health, peace of mind, financial security, support systems, and resilience—begins to crumble. Through decades of working with families, I've learned a profound truth: no estate plan, no matter how meticulously crafted, can survive unprepared heirs and broken connections.

The truth about family wealth and connection lies not far below the surface, waiting to be discovered. Like a treasure hidden in plain sight, the elements of lasting family harmony are readily accessible—not through some magical formula, but through intentional practices and deeper understanding.

What does a thriving family look like? Picture a family culture where:

- Communication flows openly and honestly
- Different perspectives are welcomed, not feared
- Conflicts become opportunities for growth
- Financial decisions align with shared values
- Each generation feels prepared and empowered

In my experience, families typically fall into three categories: those who feel confident in their preparation and connection, those who believe their situations are beyond repair, and the vast majority who exist somewhere in between—uncertain of the path forward but hoping for better. This book is for all three groups, but especially for that middle ground where small changes can yield transformative results.

In the chapters ahead, we'll explore how any family—regardless of their starting point—can build deeper connections and create lasting legacies. We'll begin by examining what happens when family bonds break down, not to dwell in the darkness, but to illuminate the path forward. Through stories, research, and practical guidance, you'll discover how to transform your family's approach to wealth, communication, and legacy planning. Remember: while this book may start by acknowledging challenges, its heart beats with hope and possibility for all families willing to take the journey.

PART I
THE FOUNDATIONS OF LEGACY

WHEN CONNECTION BREAKS

Understanding the Human
Cost of Family Disconnection

The profound impact of family disconnection isn't just a recent phenomenon. Nearly 100 years ago, renowned anthropologist Margaret Mead observed:

> *"When a death occurs in a healthy society, all the people come together. There is no need for fear or mistrust, because everyone knows what is expected of them. The funeral is a time for people to mourn together, and to support each other through their grief. But in a broken society, death is a time of fear and confusion. People don't know what to do, and they don't trust each other. This can lead to chaos and violence."*

Mead's insight resonates deeply with my own experience—both personal and professional. Let me share my story...

My Personal Story

The night before my thirtieth birthday, I lay alone in my studio apartment, four hundred miles from my dying mother. The distance felt like an ocean. At fifty-three, she wasn't supposed to leave this world yet. Not like this. Not tonight. The doctors had been clear: she probably wouldn't survive until morning.

At 2 AM, I jolted awake, my heart hammering against my ribs. Panic clawed at my throat—that primal fear of being utterly alone, of losing your primary anchor in the world. The anxiety attack gripped me like a vice, refusing to let go as hours crawled by. By 5 AM, exhausted and afraid, I drove myself to Stanford Hospital's emergency room. The doctor's advice was simple but profound: 'Find someone to talk to.'

Looking back now, I realize that night marked the beginning of two transformative themes that would shape not only my life but the lives of countless families I would later help. First was the stark recognition of our primal need for connection. Second was the critical importance of thoughtful estate planning and heir preparation a lesson that would come at a devastating personal cost.

My mother had been my anchor, my cheerleader, my best friend. She celebrated my academic achievements, comforted me through years of ear problems and multiple surgeries, and provided the steady ground beneath my feet. When she died, I lost more than a parent—I lost my sense of security and connection to the world.

The divorce of my parents when I was five had already left deep scars, their mutual bitterness creating an unbridgeable chasm. When my mother passed, I had no functional family to turn to, no shared shoulder to cry on. My two closest friends were unavailable, leaving me to navigate the stormy waters of grief alone.

Survival instinct kicked in. Within weeks, I found a roommate, started therapy, and threw myself into work as a distraction. Later, I discovered the healing power of community through ham radio and men's work—joining a core team that would meet weekly for eighteen years. These connections became my new lifeline, creating an emotional safety net that allowed me to take the risks necessary for growth and independence.

But the second theme—the importance of legacy planning—emerged from an even more painful chapter.

After my mother's death, her estate plan unraveled like a poorly knitted sweater. My brother, struggling with substance abuse and behavioral issues, became my adversary in court as we fought over asset conservation and fairness. That was forty years ago, and I haven't seen or spoken with him since. The public accusations, lies, and threats he hurled still echo in my memory.

Then came the final blow: our grandmother's death. She left her entire fortune—tens of millions of dollars—to charity, explaining that she 'didn't like the way family members were turning out.' Though personally disappointed, I was thankful for my nascent career in investments and financial planning that allowed me to stand on my own feet.

The revelation that would change my life's direction came years later while reading a book called *Preparing Heirs*. Like a bolt of lightning, it struck me: with proper mentoring and healthy connection, my family's story could have unfolded entirely differently. What if we had been taught family values around money's role and meaning? What if we had received education in financial literacy? What if we had built trust before losing our parents?

These questions led me to a profound truth: the successful transfer of wealth isn't just about documents and numbers—it's about preparing the hearts and minds of each generation. *No estate plan, however meticulously crafted, can survive unprepared heirs.*

This pivotal insight led me to my calling. Today, I help families avoid the pitfalls that can haunt them for generations. Through my work in intergenerational legacy planning and mediation, I guide families toward preserving not just their wealth, but their relationships and values.

Think of family legacy as a garden that requires constant tending. The seeds of connection, understanding, and mutual care are best planted early and nurtured consistently. Without this cultivation, even the most abundant garden can wither into a wasteland of broken relationships and squandered resources.

My story is not unique. In every community, families struggle with these same challenges. But there is hope. Through the pages of this book, I'll share the tools and wisdom I've gathered over decades of helping families navigate these waters. Together, we'll explore how to create a legacy that transcends mere wealth—one that nurtures connection, understanding, and the joy of shared purpose across generations.

The journey begins with a simple truth: your family's legacy is too important to leave to chance. Let's discover how to protect and nurture it, together. And while this book begins by calling attention to problems and challenges, remember this: the overwhelming message it contains is one of hope for all of us.

2

IGNORANCE IS NOT BLISS

The Hidden Dangers in Traditional Estate Planning

The Unseen Dangers Ahead

Every year, countless families who believe they're prepared for generational wealth transfer are walking into unseen dangers. Following conventional wisdom and practices, they focus almost solely on legal documents and tax strategies, while remaining largely unaware of the human element that ultimately determines success or failure. They've checked all the technical boxes but missed the warning signs that could signal family devastation, or lead to joyful, regenerative lives.

I've witnessed this pattern repeatedly in my decades of practice: A parent passes away, leaving behind what appears to be a meticulously crafted estate plan. The documents are perfectly drafted, the tax strategies are sound, and the administrative details are in place. Yet within months—sometimes even weeks—the family begins to unravel.

Why? Because when the distribution phase begins, there's often no one left to guide the rising generation or mediate disagreements. There's no clear understanding of the intentions behind the estate plan's structure. Old wounds, long buried under the surface, suddenly reopen. Siblings who haven't truly communicated in years find themselves forced to make joint decisions. Mutual trust deteriorates. Suspicion grows. Years of careful planning crumble in the face of human emotion and family dynamics that were never addressed.

The Hidden Tragedy

The tragedy is that by the time these issues surface, it's often too late. The family patriarch or matriarch—often the glue that held everything together—is no longer there to explain their intentions or help resolve conflicts. Without preparation, without guided practice in family decision-making, without a shared understanding of the family's values and legacy, even the most technically perfect estate plan can become a catalyst for family destruction.

This isn't just about money. When estate transitions fail, they can destroy relationships that span generations. I've seen siblings who once shared childhood memories and family dinners become permanently estranged. I've witnessed cousins who grew up playing together turn into strangers. *The cost in broken relationships often far exceeds any financial losses.*

But here's the most important thing to understand: these failures are not inevitable. They're not random acts of family misfortune. They're the predictable result of a fundamental mistake in how we approach legacy planning. The mistake is believing that proper documentation alone equals proper preparation.

The Real Reasons Plans Fail

Most people believe estate plans fail due to poor legal documentation or tax planning. This widely-held misconception leads families to focus overwhelming attention on technical details while neglecting the true drivers of success or failure. The reality, supported by decades of research and professional experience, is far more complex—and far more human.

The most comprehensive studies of failed wealth transfers reveal a startling truth: technical failures account for less than 15% of unsuccessful transitions. The real culprits? A triad of human factors that rarely receive adequate attention during the planning process:

- The Trust and Communication Breakdown. When families maintain secrets about wealth or avoid difficult conversations, they create an environment where suspicion flourishes. Children sense the unspoken tensions but learn not to ask questions. By the time the estate plan takes effect, family members lack the experience of having honest conversations about money and values.

- The Unprepared Heir Problem. Many parents, hoping to prevent their children from becoming "spoiled," avoid discussing family wealth entirely. Yet this approach backfires spectacularly. Without mentoring in financial responsibility, family values, and collaborative decision-making, heirs remain perpetual adolescents in matters of wealth—regardless of their age or success in other areas of life.

- The Missing Mission. Perhaps most devastating is the lack of a clearly articulated family mission. When there's no shared understanding of the family's purpose, values, and goals, money becomes purely transactional. Each heir pursues their own direction, often at cross-purposes with their siblings. The carefully crafted estate plan, rather than unifying the family, becomes a battlefield for competing visions.

Warning Signs and Missed Opportunities

What makes these failures particularly tragic is their predictability. The warning signs are almost always present years before the crisis erupts:

- Family gatherings where money is never discussed

- Children who reach adulthood without understanding their future responsibilities
- Siblings who haven't practiced making decisions together
- Parents who believe "the kids (or the lawyers) will sort it out" after they're gone
- Family members who avoid conflict rather than learning to navigate it constructively

Yet here's what's truly remarkable: families who *successfully* navigate wealth transitions often face the very same challenges. *The difference lies not in the absence of problems, but in how they prepare for and address them*. These families understand that estate planning is not an event but a process—one that involves the whole family in building the skills, trust, inclusion, and shared vision necessary for long-term success.

A Culture of Disconnection

The challenges facing our families don't exist in isolation. They're symptoms of a larger cultural crisis—one that the U.S. Surgeon General has identified as America's leading killer: loneliness. We live in a society that has systematically prioritized efficiency over empathy, productivity over presence, and financial security over human connection.

Think about it: When was the last time you saw "strengthening interpersonal bonds" listed as a key performance indicator? When did you last hear of a major policy initiative focused on deepening human connection? In our rush to build wealth, ensure national security, and maximize convenience, we've lost touch with something fundamental to human thriving: our need for authentic connection—to ourselves, to others, and to even to the natural world around us.

The Cost of Cultural Disconnection

This isn't just feel-good philosophy. Connection is as vital to human well-being as water and sunlight are to plants. It provides the grounding and nervous system regulation we need to function at our best. Without it, we become like trees with shallow roots—vulnerable to every storm that passes through our lives.

The impact on family legacy planning is profound. How can we expect to create meaningful inheritance plans when we're disconnected from our own values and needs? How can we prepare the next generation when we ourselves are struggling with the very connection skills they'll need to succeed?

Yet here's where hope enters the story: We're all in this together. Every person you meet—from the distant relative who never calls to the business partner who seems coldly rational—is operating within this same culture of disconnection. We've all been shaped by a society that rarely models deep connection, rarely teaches us how to cultivate it, and rarely acknowledges its fundamental importance to human flourishing.

Finding Hope in Understanding

This universal challenge points to a powerful solution: the gift of understanding. That family member who seems impossible to work with? They're likely struggling with the same yearning for connection, even if they can't name it. The parent who never taught you about money? They were probably never taught themselves. The sibling who seems only interested in their share of the inheritance? They too are a product of a culture that values financial worth over human connection.

Understanding this broader context doesn't excuse harmful behavior, but it does point us toward solutions. Just as we can learn technical skills like financial management, we can rediscover and cultivate our *innate aptitude* for connection. This innate aptitude lives in every person at every stage of life. Out of it, we can create dynamic family cultures that buck the broad societal trend, fostering the deep bonds and shared understanding that make successful legacy planning possible. *Not only that, but we ourselves get to experience the profound joy of greater emotional safety, creativity, and resourcefulness that comes with expressing our connection skills.*

The Path Forward

The chapters ahead will show you how. You'll discover practical tools for rebuilding connection, frameworks for understanding family dynamics, and strategies for creating the kind of legacy that transcends mere financial inheritance. Most importantly, you'll learn how to transform your family's relationship with wealth from a potential source of division into a powerful catalyst for connection.

Because here's the truth that decades of working with families has taught me: While our culture of disconnection has created enormous challenges, it has also created unprecedented opportunities. Every family that chooses to prioritize connection, every parent who learns to mentor rather than merely provide, every sibling group that learns to work together despite their differences—they're not just preserving their own legacy. They're helping to build a new culture, one relationship at a time. One of power, purpose, and joy.

Your family's journey toward stronger connection and meaningful legacy starts here. Welcome! Let's begin...

3

KEY PRINCIPLES

Building Blocks for
Family Connection and Legacy

Human beings, much like the physical world, operate under fundamental principles—in this case, principles that govern well-being. These principles, akin to the laws of physics, suggest that when our basic needs are met, we flourish. Beyond the essentials of air, water, food, and shelter, our primary human requirements are safety and connection. These needs, when fulfilled, unlock profound and positive qualities—awareness, empathy, creativity, joy, health, and an intrinsic drive to contribute to others.

The Primacy of Connection – A Universal Need

Connection is the cornerstone of human life. When we experience deep and meaningful connections—whether with family, friends, or community—we feel whole. Connection is not just emotional; it has profound physical, psychological, and social implications. Studies in interpersonal neurobiology by Dr. Dan Siegel reveal that strong relationships promote neural integration, fostering resilience, emotional balance, and the capacity to navigate life's challenges with grace.

When connection falters, however, vulnerability arises. Families fractured by miscommunication or mistrust often find their wealth—financial and emotional—diminished. Strong, healthy connections provide the foundation for preparing heirs to navigate and sustain family legacies.

Connection and Safety in Practice – The Five Capitals

Jay Hughes' work introduces the crucial concept of the "Five Capitals"—human, intellectual, social, spiritual, and financial. His research emphasizes that financial capital should always be subordinated to the development of the other four capitals within a family. His reasoning is simple but profound: money is a tool, not the purpose of a thriving, multi-generational family.

Why financial capital belongs at the bottom of the Five Capitals:

1. Money Without Capability is a Liability. If financial capital (wealth) is placed at the top, it can lead to entitlement, dependency, and family discord. Wealth that is not paired with strong personal development, knowledge, and relationships can erode a family over generations, rather than sustaining it.

2. The True Source of Wealth is People, Not Dollars. The real foundation of multi-generational success is human capital—the well-being, talents, values, and emotional intelligence of family members. When families invest in their people first, they create a legacy that can adapt, grow, and sustain wealth meaningfully.

3. Intellectual and Social Capital Create a Stronger Family Enterprise. A family that values intellectual capital (education, skills, critical thinking) and social capital (trust, relationships, reputation) is far more likely to use financial wealth wisely. Without these, inherited wealth often leads to poor decisions, conflicts, and dissipation of resources.

4. Spiritual Capital Gives Money Purpose. Spiritual capital (which is not necessarily religious but reflects values, purpose, and shared vision) provides a guiding framework for how a family uses its resources. Families that lack a strong sense of purpose often see their wealth fragment within a generation or two.

5. Wealth Lasts When It Serves the Family, Not the Other Way Around. Placing money at the top forces a family to chase and defend wealth rather than use it as a tool for growth and well-being. When financial capital is at the bottom, it becomes a servant to the family's greater mission, ensuring that wealth serves people rather than people serving wealth.

Think of building a great estate: If you start with gold bricks (money) but no foundation (family development, knowledge, and values), the house will eventually crumble. But if you build a strong foundation—by developing capable, connected, and purposeful family members—then the wealth becomes a tool to sustain the house over generations rather than something that threatens to bury it.

The Role of Purposeful Planning

Purposeful planning practices emphasize that true legacy planning is not solely about distributing assets but about preserving relationships. David York's insights on integrating personal stories and values into estate planning highlight the importance of fostering connection as an intentional practice.

Families that engage in collaborative decision-making, storytelling, and shared rituals strengthen their bonds and can create a legacy rooted in love and mutual respect.

Connection First – Lessons from Nature

Jon Young's teachings on nature connection offer a profound metaphor (and training ground) for human relationships. In nature, interdependence is a survival strategy. Similarly, families flourish when members recognize their interconnectedness and cultivate curiosity about one another's experiences.

Practices like storytelling, reflective listening, and shared outdoor experiences can rekindle dormant connections. By engaging in these practices, families mirror the rhythms of nature—building awareness, responding to change, nurturing growth, and finding resilience in adversity.

The Costs of Disconnection – The Information Vacuum

Disconnection often arises from a lack of information. When families fail to communicate openly, misunderstandings and mistrust tend to proliferate. The vacuum created by silence can be filled with assumptions and fears. This is our brain's default state: protecting us from (real and imagined) danger. After all, it was our ancestors who ran from danger first who survived, as the story goes. As a result, we all have generous amounts of "fear DNA," which leads to conflict (fight or flight).

Collaborative Practice, championed by pioneers such as Nancy Ross, addresses this issue by fostering facilitated, respectful communication in an emotionally safe team mediation setting. It's an example of a proven approach that can help restore connection even in the most challenging of family conflicts. It ensures that every voice is heard respectfully, enabling families to find solutions that honor their collective needs and values.

Toward a Flourishing Future – The Power of Positive Attributes

When connection and safety are prioritized, families naturally exhibit qualities that enhance their collective well-being. Empathy, creativity, and a spirit of helpfulness emerge organically. These attributes not only strengthen families but also empower them to contribute positively to their communities.

As Jon Young observes, "What we understand and invest in becomes an extension of ourselves." When families invest in their relationships, they create a virtuous ripple effect that extends far beyond their immediate circles in space and time.

Practical Implementation – Making It Real

The principles outlined above aren't just theoretical—they can be actively cultivated through specific practices:

1. Regular Family Gatherings
   - Structured time for sharing and listening
   - Space for both celebration and addressing challenges
   - Inclusion of all generations

2. Intentional Communication
   - Active listening practices
   - Recognition of each person's unique perspective
   - Regular check-ins between gatherings

3. Shared Experiences
   - Family rituals and traditions
   - Collaborative projects
   - Learning opportunities together

4. Safety-Building Practices
   - Establishing clear boundaries and expectations
   - Predictable responses to vulnerability
   - Consistent follow-through on commitments

Conclusion: Connection as the Foundation

The principles outlined in this chapter form the foundation for thriving families and communities. By prioritizing safety and connection, we unlock the innate potential within each family member to grow, contribute, and thrive. These aren't just nice ideas—they're essential elements for creating and sustaining meaningful family legacies.

Consider the following principles of Regenerative Family Design as tools that can be utilized in service of your family's well-being and future:

- Safety creates the environment for growth
- Connection provides the structural support

- Values guide healthier decision-making
- Communication maintains relationships
- Shared experiences build lasting bonds

As we move forward to explore specific strategies and tools in the coming chapters, remember that these core principles underlie all successful family systems. Whether you're just beginning to think about legacy planning, or working to strengthen existing family bonds, these fundamentals can help guide your path forward.

In the next chapter, we'll dive deeper into the critical elements of safety and trust—exploring how to create the secure foundation necessary for authentic connection and meaningful legacy planning. You'll discover practical tools for fostering the kind of environment where family members can truly thrive.

PART II
WHAT PEOPLE NEED

4

SAFETY AND TRUST

Creating the Foundation
for Authentic Family Relationships

The Courage to Connect

During a recent men's retreat in the mountains of Northern California, I witnessed a profound demonstration of how safety transforms human interaction. Fifty men, mostly strangers to each other, gathered in a circle on the first evening. The facilitator began by sharing a deeply personal story of loss and redemption. His vulnerability created an invisible shield of safety around the group. One by one, men who had arrived guarded and hesitant began sharing their own stories—of fathers they couldn't please, of children they struggled to understand, of legacies they hoped to build or repair, of shame and fear.

This experience crystallized what decades of research in psychology and neuroscience have shown: when people feel safe, they can access parts of themselves usually hidden behind walls of reactivity. In families, this principle becomes even more crucial. The stakes are higher, the histories more complex and entrenched, and the potential for both healing and harm more significant.

To illustrate the profound impact of creating a safe and supportive environment, let me share a personal experience that transformed my understanding of trust and connection.

When I was five years old, my father beat my mother. What I remember is that I was lying in bed at night and I heard them arguing loudly in the living room. At some point, I heard the sound of hands hitting flesh, slapping I suppose. Hard. I was starkly afraid that my father was going to kill my mother. I knew about his strong temper, but I couldn't see what was going on, which made it all the more frightening. I cried out for them to stop, and eventually my father poked his head into my room and told me everything was okay, and to go back to sleep. Of course I couldn't go back to sleep. And after what seemed an eternity, my mother came in and sat down on my bed next to me. I'll never forget her face, which was swollen on one side and on that side, her eye was blood red. My heart was broken. The next morning I woke up to a policeman in the house and no father. For many, many years, I mistrusted men, but it went deeper than that. I believed, deep in my guts, that if a group of men, say five or more, were together for even a couple of hours, that a physical fight would break out, and I never wanted to be in that position.

Why am I telling you this? Because I want you to understand that fear, mistrust, and trauma can be healed quickly under the right circumstances.

You see, decades later, when I was in my early 40s, I was at a difficult point of choice in my life. A close friend and colleague, who was a mentor to me, suggested that I attend a mens' personal growth weekend. I trusted him, and I was at my wits end with the choice I had been wrestling with. He said that the experience might help me get through it and finally get some clarity. I was pretty much desperate enough to try anything, so I signed up. The gathering was to start early in the morning on Saturday, and the night before, I did not sleep. At all. Fear and anxiety really put me through the wringer. The prospect of two and a half days locked in a big room with 300 men? Every fiber in my body went on high alert during the night and wouldn't let me rest. But at 5:00am, I dragged my sorry self out of bed, got ready, and drove to the Masonic Hall, where the event was being held.

That morning, magic happened, and my life has never been the same. What I experienced, in a nutshell, was men stepping up to lead with courage and love. With respect and honor. Men supported each other in authentic, bedrock terms — verbally, emotionally, and physically. There was no mistaking it, I was supported by every man in that room. and by the end of the first day, I was overcome with joy. And without doubt, I was a man among men. That Saturday, I fell in love with men.

I don't want you to miss this key point: decades of trauma and fear can be overcome in as little as a day. Relationships can be healed rapidly under the right circumstances.

That experience led me to join what we called a men's "team," in our case seven men who met around a fire, outside, every Thursday night for 18 years. And that emotional support, deep listening, and caring gave me the emotionally stable ground (I believe we all need) to stand on and move my life forward. I could write an entire book about that team journey, but you may already see where I'm headed here. For the price of some discomfort upfront, we can step through unseen doors into new worlds of connection that leave us changed forever. In terms of families and legacy, that experience and the years that followed taught me a lifetime of lessons about human belonging, about deep listening, about emotional safety, about my own gifts, about standing up and taking my rightful place in the world, and so much more.

Just as I found healing and connection through the men's weekend, families can create similar environments of safety and trust that foster deeper connections and understanding. My advice is, get professional assistance if needed. A skilled communications coach or mediator from outside the family can work wonders.

The Science of Safety

Our brains are exquisitely tuned to detect threats in our environment. Dr. Stephen Porges's Polyvagal Theory explains how our nervous system continuously scans for signals of danger or security. When we sense threat—whether physical or emotional—our body prepares for fight, flight, or freeze. Blood flow shifts away from our prefrontal cortex (the thinking brain) toward systems necessary for survival. This biological response made perfect sense when our ancestors faced physical dangers, but it can become problematic in family discussions about wealth, legacy, or difficult group decisions.

When we feel safe, our nervous system enters what Porges calls a state of "social engagement." Our heart rate variability increases, promoting emotional regulation. Our facial muscles relax, making us more expressive and receptive. Even our middle ear muscles adjust, specifically tuning to human voice frequencies. Perhaps most importantly, our prefrontal cortex engages fully, allowing access to our highest reasoning abilities. These physiological changes create the conditions necessary for meaningful connection, creative problem-solving, and genuine empathy.

The Foundation of Trust

Safety — or the lack of it — forms the foundation upon which all other family dynamics rest. Without it, even the most carefully crafted estate plans or family governance structures can crumble. When family members don't feel safe expressing their thoughts or feelings, important information remains hidden, resentments build silently, and collaborative decision-making becomes impossible. The family's collective wisdom remains untapped, locked behind walls of fear and self-protection.

Building psychological safety in families requires intentional effort and understanding. It begins with creating what we might call "containers of safety"—environments and interactions where people know their voices matter and their vulnerabilities won't be used against them. This happens in relatively predictable environments or contexts, where emotional reactions can remain mostly low-key, and agreements are consistently honored. It grows through non-judgmental listening, where family members feel heard without criticism and questions come from genuine curiosity rather than accusation.

The theme of harmony as a shared value echoes through countless traditions and cultures, though it is known by many names: shalom, maluhia, sacred silence, and the "plane of possibility."

The role of family leadership proves crucial in this process. When parents or elder family members demonstrate vulnerability and openness—showing willingness to admit mistakes, receive feedback, and express genuine curiosity about others' perspectives—they create permission for everyone to show up more authentically. *This modeling effect can transform family culture more powerfully than any formal policy or procedure.*

Breaking Through Fear Barriers

Fear serves as the primary obstacle to establishing safety in families. People often carry deep-seated fears of judgment or rejection, of losing control or status, of conflict or confrontation, or simply of making mistakes and appearing foolish. These fears manifest in defensive communication, avoidance of important conversations, rigid adherence to roles or patterns, and resistance to change or new ideas.

The journey through these fears begins with small steps. Families can find success when they start with lower-stakes conversations, practicing vulnerability in manageable doses. Simple communication protocols can help, such as taking turns speaking without interruption and reflecting back what others have said before responding. Regular family check-ins provide opportunities to build these skills gradually, creating space for both celebration and concern.

The Power of Authentic Presence

Safety emerges not just from what we say or do, but from how we show up with each other. Authentic presence involves being fully attentive to the present moment, maintaining emotional regulation, demonstrating genuine interest in others, and responding with empathy and understanding. This quality of presence can't be faked—people, especially family members, have finely tuned sensors for authenticity.

Cultivating this kind of presence requires practice. It means developing mindful awareness of our own emotional states and paying attention to non-verbal cues. It involves learning to regulate our emotions, taking breaks when needed, and modeling healthy emotional expression. Perhaps most importantly, it requires the art of deep listening—focusing fully on the speaker without planning our response, and asking questions from genuine curiosity rather than assumption.

Pro tip: Acknowledge at the outset that ithis journey toward authenticity is new, and that you—along with your other family members—will occasionally stumble or fall back on old habits. Establishing it as okay models being authentic, and builds trust.

The Journey Toward Trust

Building safety and trust in families is not a destination but a continuing journey. It requires consistent attention, regular maintenance, and ongoing learning and adjustment. As safety grows, families often experience more honest communication, better decision-making, stronger bonds across generations, and greater resilience in facing challenges.

Even in the most conscious families, breaches of safety will occur. The key lies not in preventing all breaches but in how they're repaired. Quick recognition of the breach, clear steps toward repair, and integration of the learning prove essential.

When family members acknowledge impacts promptly, take responsibility regardless of intent, and make specific amends, trust can actually grow stronger.

The Legacy of Safety

When families create genuine psychological safety, they lay the groundwork for successful wealth transitions, meaningful legacy planning, authentic relationships, and collective wisdom and growth. The investment in building safety pays dividends far beyond any financial inheritance. It creates an emotional and social legacy that strengthens families for generations to come.

Every interaction either builds or erodes safety. By making conscious choices about how we show up with family members, we contribute to a culture where trust can flourish and genuine connection can thrive. This invisible foundation—more valuable than any tangible asset—becomes the true treasure we pass on to future generations.

The practice of creating safety requires patience, commitment, and courage. It asks us to be vulnerable when we'd rather protect ourselves, to listen when we'd rather speak, and to stay present when we'd rather withdraw. Yet the rewards—deeper connections, more authentic relationships, and a family culture that nurtures growth—make every effort worthwhile. In the end, the safety we create becomes the soil from which all other family possibilities grow.

5

INCLUSION AND TRANSPARENCY

Building Trust Through Openness

A family sits around their dining room table, tension thick in the air. The youngest daughter has just asked about the family's estate plans, and her question hangs heavy in the silence. The parents exchange worried glances, wondering how much to share. The older siblings shift uncomfortably, some already knowing pieces of information others don't. This scene, played out in countless homes, illustrates a crucial crossroads many families face: the choice between openness and secrecy, between inclusion and exclusion.

The Power of Being an Insider

Human beings share a fundamental need to belong. When we're excluded from important family discussions or decisions, particularly those that affect our future, our nervous systems naturally react with a sense of threat. This biological response makes perfect sense from an evolutionary standpoint—in our ancestors' time, exclusion from the tribe could mean death. While the stakes may seem less dire today, our brains and bodies still respond to exclusion as if our survival were at risk.

Consider what happens when family members are kept in the dark about important decisions or plans. Their minds begin filling the information void with assumptions, often assuming worst-case scenarios. Anxiety rises, trust erodes, and family members may seek information from unreliable sources or form informal alliances based on incomplete understanding. Even when nothing improper is occurring, the mere fact of exclusion can damage relationships in ways that take years to repair.

Conversely, when people feel included and have access to appropriate information, they experience a sense of security that allows them to engage more constructively with others. Dr. Dan Siegel's research in interpersonal neurobiology demonstrates that inclusion activates neural pathways associated with safety and trust. When we feel like valued insiders, our capacity for rational thinking, empathy, and collaborative problem-solving expands dramatically.

Creating Safe Spaces for Dialogue

The practice of inclusion requires more than simply having everyone in the same room. It demands the creation of an environment where all voices are welcomed and valued. Drawing from my experience in Collaborative Practice, I've witnessed how families transform when they establish ground rules for communication and ensure equal speaking opportunities. These aren't just polite suggestions—they're essential tools for building the kind of safety that allows authentic dialogue to emerge.

In one example, an early teen sat by an outdoor fire with other boys his age, but he stood out. The other boys were used to the outdoors and camaraderie, but this particular young man came from a tough neighborhood and was new to the group. He sat with headphones on, a hoodie pulled down over his face, his body language clearly indicating his withdrawal from the group. The others, wise beyond their years, didn't say or do anything. This is what we call "a culture of allowance," where individuals are free to be themselves with no overt judgement or shaming. Over the ensuing hours and days, he gradually emerged from his "shell," and became one of the strongest contributors to the group. A respected elder, who had pretty much given up on mentoring youth, later met this young man, and shared that he thought this particular young man was worthy of being a leader, and expressed his willingness to personally be his mentor.

I recall working with one family where the eldest son had always dominated conversations, often interrupting his quieter siblings. Through structured family meetings with clear communication protocols, they discovered that the youngest daughter—usually silent in family gatherings—had valuable insights about modernizing the family business. Her perspective, previously overshadowed, ended up launching a successful digital transformation initiative that benefited everyone.

The Role of Information Access

Transparency goes hand-in-hand with inclusion, acting as its practical expression in family systems. When family members have access to relevant information about family assets, plans, and decision-making processes, they become empowered participants rather than passive observers. This doesn't mean everyone needs to know every detail of every decision, but it does mean creating clear channels for sharing appropriate information and explaining why certain things might need to remain confidential.

The key lies in finding the right balance. Consider the story of the Ramirez family, who transformed their approach to family communication after nearly losing their business to internal conflict. They instituted regular family meetings with clear agendas, created secure ways to share important documents, and established protocols for requesting additional information. Most importantly, they made sure everyone understood not just what decisions were being made, but why and how they aligned with the family's values and goals.

Building Trust Through Belonging

Drawing from John Powell's (who spells his name in lowercase in the belief that we should be "part of the universe, not over it, as capitals signify") groundbreaking work on belonging and bridging, we can understand family inclusion through a deeper lens. As Powell teaches, belonging is a fundamental human need that goes beyond mere inclusion — it's about being fully seen and accepted as a co-creator of shared spaces and experiences.

The Difference Between Inclusion and Belonging

Powell makes an important distinction between simple inclusion and true belonging. In families, mere inclusion might mean inviting everyone to holiday gatherings or copying all members on financial updates. But belonging, as Powell defines it, requires a deeper transformation where each family member feels they can authentically shape the family's culture, decisions, and future.

Consider a family meeting where younger generations are "included" but don't feel empowered to influence outcomes. Powell would argue this falls short of true belonging, which requires what he calls "co-creation" — where all members help define what the family means and how it operates.

Breaking Down Othering in Families

Powell's concept of "othering" — the systematic marginalization of people perceived as different — can manifest within families in subtle ways:

- The "black sheep" sibling who's technically included but emotionally distanced
- In-laws who are invited but not truly integrated into decision-making
- Children who are seen but not heard in important family discussions

To counter this, Powell advocates for "bridging" — maintaining proximity and curiosity toward those we perceive as different. In family contexts, this means:

- Active listening across generational divides
- Seeking to understand different perspectives on family wealth and legacy
- Creating spaces where all members can share fears and hopes

The Structure of Belonging

Powell emphasizes that belonging requires both cultural and structural change. For families, this means:

- Cultural Elements:
    - Shared storytelling that includes all voices

    - Recognition of multiple family identities and experiences
    - Celebration of diverse contributions to family success

- Structural Elements:
    - Clear pathways for participation in decision-making
    - Transparent access to family information
    - Formal roles that distribute power and responsibility

Creating Transformative Spaces

Powell's work on "targeted universalism" - setting universal goals while acknowledging different groups need different approaches - can guide family inclusion strategies. This might mean:

- Recognizing that younger family members may need different types of support to participate meaningfully
- Understanding that in-laws bring valuable outside perspectives that need specific channels for expression
- Acknowledging that family members with different financial circumstances may need different forms of engagement

The Role of Bridging

As Powell teaches, bridging isn't about eliminating differences but about creating connections across them. In families, this means:

- Maintaining curiosity about different viewpoints rather than demanding agreement
- Creating safe spaces for difficult conversations
- Building relationships before tackling contentious issues

Moving Beyond Fear

Powell's insights about how fear drives othering apply powerfully to family dynamics. When families face changes — whether through marriage, divorce, inheritance, or business transitions — fear can lead to exclusionary behaviors. The antidote, according to Powell, is creating what he calls "circles of human concern" that expand rather than contract during stress.

Practical Implementation

Drawing from Powell's frameworks, families can build belonging through:

- Regular check-ins that go beyond surface updates to deeper sharing
- Rotating leadership roles in family meetings
- Creating multiple channels for input and feedback

- Establishing clear processes for raising concerns
- Building in reflection time to examine family patterns

The Path Forward

As Powell reminds us, belonging is both a destination and a practice. Families must continually work at creating spaces where all members feel they truly belong without requiring others to be othered. This means staying vigilant about power dynamics, maintaining openness to change, and regularly examining whether structures and practices serve everyone's needs.

Through this lens of belonging, family inclusion becomes not just about who gets invited to the table, but about creating a table where everyone helps decide what's served and how it's shared.

Remember: The goal isn't perfect harmony but authentic engagement across differences. As Powell teaches, true belonging emerges when we can bring our full selves to our relationships while making space for others to do the same. The Chen family offers an illuminating example. When planning their family foundation's future, they took time to explore each family member's philanthropic interests, even those that seemed far from the foundation's traditional focus areas. This process revealed unexpected synergies between the younger generation's passion for environmental causes and the elder generation's interest in community development. By fully honoring and including these diverse perspectives, they created an innovative grant-making program that engaged everyone, while amplifying their impact.

The Preventive Power of Regular Communication

Regular, structured communication serves as a powerful protective measure against misunderstandings and conflicts. Even brief updates can reassure family members that nothing significant has changed, provide opportunities to ask questions before concerns grow, and maintain connection during busy periods. This ongoing dialogue builds habits of openness that serve families well during both calm times and crises. It also serves to naturally attenuate false and disruptive narratives.

Think of communication like tending a garden. Regular attention—watering, weeding, pruning—keeps the garden healthy and productive. Neglect it, and weeds of misunderstanding and disconnect begin to take over. Just as a garden needs consistent care rather than occasional intense intervention, family communication thrives on regular attention rather than crisis-driven discussions.

Navigating Practical Challenges

Of course, implementing these principles in real family life presents practical challenges. Geographic distance, different communication styles, complex information, and time constraints can all complicate the process of maintaining transparency and inclusion. Yet families who commit to these *values* find creative ways to overcome these obstacles.

For geographically dispersed families, technology offers powerful tools for maintaining connection. Regular video calls, secure document sharing platforms, and digital family newsletters can help bridge physical distances. However, it's crucial to remember that technology should enhance, not replace, meaningful human interaction. Many families find success in combining regular virtual check-ins with less frequent but more substantial in-person gatherings.

The Impact on Legacy Planning

When inclusion and transparency become embedded in family culture, estate planning transforms from a potentially divisive process into an opportunity for strengthening family bonds. Plans are better understood because everyone has contributed to their development. Family members feel more prepared for their future roles because they've been included in discussions and decisions along the way. Perhaps most importantly, relationships remain stronger because the planning process has reinforced rather than strained family connections.

Consider the contrast between two approaches to legacy planning. In one common scenario, parents work with advisors to create an estate plan in isolation, revealing its details only after death or incapacity. This approach, while perhaps well-intentioned, often leads to confusion, hurt feelings, and potential conflict when the plan finally comes to light. In contrast, families who embrace inclusion and transparency can engage in ongoing dialogue about the thinking behind their planning decisions, allowing for questions, concerns, and suggestions to be addressed while everyone can still participate in the conversation.

Measuring Success

The success of inclusion and transparency initiatives shows up in subtle but significant ways. Family members begin voluntarily participating in discussions they previously avoided. Communication becomes more proactive rather than reactive. The frequency of surprises and conflicts decreases, while instances of collaborative problem-solving increase. Perhaps most tellingly, family members demonstrate greater resilience when facing challenges because they trust in their collective ability to work through difficulties together.

Looking Forward

As families grow and change, their practices around inclusion and transparency must evolve as well. Regular review and adjustment of communication systems helps ensure they continue serving family needs effectively. This might mean adapting meeting formats as new generations join the family, updating information-sharing platforms as technology changes, or modifying decision-making processes as the family's circumstances evolve.

Conclusion

Inclusion and transparency are not just nice-to-have features of family dynamics; they are *essential elements* for preserving relationships and resources across generations. By making these principles central to family operations, we create the conditions for trust, understanding, and successful legacy planning.

The investment in building these practices pays dividends in reduced conflict, stronger relationships, and more effective resource management. Most importantly, it helps ensure that family members feel valued, informed, and connected—the true measure of family wealth. In the end, the openness we cultivate becomes not just a practice but a legacy itself, teaching future generations the power of bringing everyone into the circle of trust and understanding.

6

ROLES IN THE FAMILY

Breaking Free from Labels

Every family carries an invisible script—a set of unwritten rules and expectations about who each member is supposed to be. These roles often emerge as shortcuts for understanding complex family dynamics, but they can become prisons that limit growth and connection. Drawing from my own story, which I shared earlier about being labeled "the responsible one" while my brother became "the troubled one," I've witnessed firsthand how these labels can create lasting damage to family relationships and contribute to the loss of connection across generations.

The Power and Peril of Family Roles

Sarah sat across from me in my office, her hands wrapped tightly around a cup of tea that had long since gone cold. "I've always been 'the responsible one,'" she said, "the achiever who made straight A's, never missed a deadline, and seemed to have her life perfectly mapped out." She paused, then added quietly, "No one ever saw the crushing anxiety behind closed doors."

Her brother Tom had been assigned a different role: "the black sheep"—struggling with direction, changing jobs frequently, and often needing financial help. What the family never recognized was Tom's brilliant creativity that emerged when he felt truly seen, or how their rigid role assignments prevented both siblings from exploring their full humanity.

The turning point came during a family legacy planning session, when their father's estate planner suggested they try something different: spending time together without their usual roles. The simple act of dropping labels opened new possibilities for connection. Using Dr. Dan Siegel's concept of "mindsight"—the ability to perceive the mind of another while being aware of our own—the siblings began seeing each other with fresh eyes.

"I never knew you felt that way," Tom said to Sarah after she revealed her private struggles with perfectionism. "I always thought you had it all figured out."

"And I never understood the pressure you felt being compared to me," Sarah responded. "I see now how that must have shaped your choices."

The Science Behind Role-Labeling

Our brains create shortcuts to manage complexity—it's a natural and necessary function of human cognition. But these shortcuts can calcify into rigid patterns that resist new information. When families assign fixed roles, they're essentially creating a closed system that resists growth and adaptation. The cost extends far beyond individual relationships.

Consider the matriarch or patriarch role—often seen as the "keeper of family wisdom." While this role can provide stability, it can also prevent new perspectives from emerging. In Sarah and Tom's family, their father's role as "the successful businessman" made it difficult for him to appreciate Tom's more creative, entrepreneurial approach to work. His identity had become so entwined with his role that considering alternative approaches felt threatening to his sense of self.

Research in family systems shows that these rigid role assignments often lead to decreased emotional intelligence within the family, reduced ability to adapt to change, and the intergenerational transmission of limiting patterns. Perhaps most painfully, they result in missed opportunities for genuine connection and stunted individual growth.

Breaking Free Through Understanding

The breakthrough for many families comes through what family therapist Virginia Satir called "temperature taking"—regularly checking in with how roles might be limiting family members' full expression. This isn't just about dropping labels; it's about creating space for complexity and growth while maintaining the stability that roles initially provided.

For Sarah and Tom's family, their facilitator introduced a process called "role exploration." Instead of simply rejecting their old roles, they began to examine them with curiosity. Sarah discovered that aspects of being "the responsible one" had served her well in her career, but she didn't have to maintain perfect control in every area of life. Tom realized that while being the "black sheep" had given him freedom to experiment, it had also kept him from committing to projects he truly cared about.

As we explored in Chapter 4, psychological safety forms the foundation for growth and change. When family members feel secure enough to experiment with new roles, they're drawing on the safety principles we discussed earlier. Just as a secure base allows children to explore their world confidently, a family environment grounded in trust and acceptance enables members to expand beyond limiting roles. This safety becomes particularly crucial when challenging long-standing family patterns.

The Dance of Change

The science of neuroplasticity tells us that our brains can and do form new patterns at every age. Dr. Siegel's research shows that secure attachments—feeling seen, safe, and valued—actually enhance our capacity for growth and change. This means families can create what we might call "dynamic stability"—maintaining connection while allowing for evolution.

Consider these common family roles and their potential for transformation: The Achiever often carries the family's success narrative but may suppress their own desires. The Mediator keeps peace but may lose touch with their own needs. The Problem Child may actually be the system's "truth teller." The Perfect One often hides significant pain or fear. The Caretaker may need care themselves but doesn't know how to receive it.

Practical Paths to Freedom

For Sarah and Tom's family, real change began when they started practicing what their facilitator called "role flexibility." This meant acknowledging the original protective function of roles, recognizing when roles no longer served, experimenting with new behaviors in a safe environment, and supporting each other through uncomfortable changes.

Their father found this especially challenging. "If I'm not the family problem-solver," he asked, "then who am I?" This common fear—that letting go of roles means losing identity—

often keeps families stuck. The answer came through practice. During family meetings, they began rotating responsibilities: sometimes Tom would take the lead on financial discussions, while Sarah practiced stepping back. Their father learned to listen without immediately offering solutions.

Navigating the Emotional Terrain

The most challenging aspect of role transformation isn't the practical changes—it's managing the emotional undertow. As their facilitator explained, "When we shift roles, we're not just changing behaviors. We're reorganizing the family's emotional field."

This became evident when Tom took the lead on restructuring their family's charitable foundation. Sarah found herself experiencing unexpected anxiety: "I should be happy he's stepping up," she confided in a private session. "But I feel like I'm disappearing. Who am I if I'm not the one holding everything together?"

Their facilitator introduced the concept of "emotional bandwidth"—the idea that families can expand their capacity for complexity gradually, like strengthening a muscle. A breakthrough came during a family retreat when their father shared vulnerably: "I've always seen Tom's creativity as a threat to our family's stability. Now I realize that was about my fears, not his capabilities. What if his different approach is exactly what our family needs?"

Sustaining Change in the Face of Stress

The real test of role transformation comes not in the initial shifts, but in maintaining flexibility over time—especially during stress or crisis. Sarah and Tom's family discovered this when their father faced a health scare. Initially, everyone snapped back to their old roles: Sarah taking charge of medical decisions, Tom feeling sidelined, their father retreating into the "strong, silent" patriarch role.

But this time, they had new tools and awareness. "I notice we're all sliding back," Sarah said during a family meeting. "Maybe that's okay for now, but let's be conscious about it." This led to what their facilitator called "role elasticity"—the ability to move between old and new patterns as circumstances required.

The Legacy of Flexibility

Five years after beginning their role transformation work, Sarah and Tom's family discovered that their changes had ripple effects far beyond individual relationships. The family's emotional and financial wealth had grown in unexpected ways. Their father reflected during a legacy planning session, "What strikes me most is how much talent we were leaving on the table with our old patterns. We were so busy protecting ourselves from imagined threats that we couldn't see our real strengths."

Perhaps most significantly, they were creating a new legacy for the next generation. Sarah's teenage daughter noticed the difference: "Mom's so much more relaxed now. And Uncle Tom—he's still fun and creative, but he follows through. They seem more... real."

Conclusion: Embracing the Full Human Story

The journey beyond limiting roles is neither quick nor easy, but its rewards extend far beyond the immediate family system. When families develop the capacity for role flexibility while maintaining strong connections, they create a legacy of emotional intelligence and adaptability that serves generations to come.

This may be the most valuable inheritance we can offer: the freedom to grow, the safety to change, and the wisdom to know that our roles need not define us. In this way, family wealth—in all its forms—becomes truly regenerative, growing and evolving with each generation's unique contributions.

While breaking free from rigid roles marks an important step in family evolution, it often stirs up underlying conflicts that have been suppressed by predictable role patterns. As we'll explore in Chapter 7, these emerging conflicts, when handled skillfully, can actually accelerate positive change. The very tension that arises from role transformation can become a catalyst for deeper understanding and more authentic relationships.

7

CONFLICT AND COMMON GROUND

Transforming Family
Challenges into Opportunities

The silence in the conference room felt heavy enough to touch. Three siblings sat around a mahogany table, their father's will spread before them, each avoiding the others' eyes. Maria, the eldest, gripped her coffee cup as if it might anchor her to earth. James, the middle child, repeatedly checked his phone, though no messages had arrived. And Sarah, the youngest, stared out the window, tears threatening to spill. Their father's estate—a family business built over forty years—had become a battlefield of competing claims and unspoken grievances.

This scene, one I've witnessed countless times in my practice, illustrates how conflict, when avoided or mishandled, can tear families apart. Yet beneath its thorny surface, conflict often conceals the seeds of transformation—a gateway to deeper understanding and stronger bonds.

The Fear That Binds Us

Fear of conflict is perhaps the most significant barrier to family reconciliation. The mere thought of confronting unresolved issues with family members often triggers feelings of anxiety, anger, shame, or humiliation. These emotions can feel so overwhelming that avoidance becomes the default response. Many families remain stuck in patterns of dysfunction because the idea of engaging in a difficult conversation feels insurmountable.

But what if we could reframe conflict? Instead of seeing it as a threat, we might view it as a bridge—a pathway to understanding and intimacy. For this shift to occur, families need both the courage to take the first step and the skills (or help) to navigate the complexities of human emotions.

This fear response connects directly to our earlier discussion of safety in Chapter 4. When family members don't feel psychologically safe, their nervous systems remain on high alert, making productive conflict resolution impossible. Similarly, the rigid roles we explored in Chapter 6 often emerge as defense mechanisms against this very fear.

As I experienced during the men's weekend, stepping into a space of vulnerability and finding unconditional support can transform fear into connection and understanding. The results can seem magical. Just as I overcame my deep-seated mistrust and found a community of support among men, families can also navigate their fears and conflicts by creating environments where open dialogue and empathy are prioritized—and the very real possibility of support can arise.

The Promise of Respectful Dispute Resolution

Collaborative Practice offers a structured, compassionate approach to resolving family disputes, even in advanced stages. Unlike adversarial methods that tend to deepen divisions regardless of the outcome, this model creates a safe space where all voices are heard and valued. By bringing together neutral professionals trained in law, finance, and communication, families can address their issues constructively. Collaborative Practice Trusts and Estates is one such process that applies and builds on these principles.

Consider the transformation of the Martinez family. After their mother's death, three siblings found themselves locked in bitter disagreement over her antique collection—pieces that carried deep emotional significance for each of them. Traditional legal approaches had only intensified their conflict. Through Collaborative Practice, they discovered that beneath their arguments about monetary value lay a shared desire to honor their mother's memory. This realization opened the door to creative solutions none had previously considered.

Just as we saw with family roles and inclusion (Chapters 5 and 6), creating a safe container for difficult conversations allows natural healing and growth to occur. The transparency principles we discussed earlier become especially crucial when navigating conflict.

The Neuroscience of Conflict

Dr. Dan Siegel's work on interpersonal neurobiology helps explain why conflict feels so threatening and how we can work with our natural responses rather than against them. Our brains are wired to react to perceived threats with a fight, flight, or freeze response. This primitive survival mechanism often escalates conflict, making it difficult to engage in rational, empathetic dialogue.

The key elements that most commonly trigger our threat response in family conflicts include:

- Perceived attacks on identity or status
- Challenges to deeply held beliefs
- Fear of loss (emotional or material)
- Threats to belonging or acceptance
- Unmet expectations or broken trust

Understanding these triggers allows us to approach conflict with greater awareness and intentionality. When we recognize our reactive patterns, we can choose more constructive responses.

The Bridge of Understanding

Jon Young's Attributes of Connection provide a powerful framework for navigating family conflict. These time-tested principles help create the conditions for genuine dialogue:

1. Curiosity before judgment
2. Self-awareness and emotional regulation
3. Empathic listening and validation
4. Recognition of shared humanity
5. Commitment to mutual growth

When families embrace these attributes, seemingly intractable conflicts often begin to shift. The key lies not in avoiding disagreement but in approaching it with a spirit of discovery and care for relationships, putting connection first.

Stories of Transformation

Let me share a story that illustrates the transformative power of addressing conflict skillfully. The Thompson family arrived in my office after years of estrangement. The catalyst? A disputed inheritance that had divided three generations. The surface issue involved a family vacation home, but beneath lay decades of unspoken grievances and misunderstandings.

Through careful facilitation, family members began to share their stories—not just about the property, but about their deeper hopes, fears, and unmet needs. Sarah, the youngest sister, revealed how excluded she felt from family decisions despite her financial expertise. Michael, the eldest brother, spoke about the crushing weight of trying to preserve their parents' legacy alone. Their mother, watching her children struggle, finally shared her own fears about the family falling apart.

The breakthrough came not through legal solutions but through a shift in how they listened to each other. When Michael truly heard Sarah's pain of exclusion, his defensive stance softened. When Sarah understood Michael's sense of isolation in carrying family responsibilities, her anger morphed into compassion. Together, they found creative ways to honor both their parents' wishes and each person's needs.

Practical Steps for Breaking the Spell of Conflict

Moving through family conflict requires courage, skill, and sometimes professional support. Here's a practical pathway forward:

1. Acknowledge your fear without letting it paralyze you
2. Seek help from trained collaborative professionals
3. Practice active listening without interrupting
4. Focus on *interests* rather than *positions*
5. Cultivate patience and empathy

The Role of Professional Support

Professional mediators, interdisciplinary Collaborative Practice teams, and family therapists can provide invaluable guidance through difficult conversations, as can properly trained facilitators from other fields, such as certain financial professionals and trustees. Their expertise helps create structure and safety for addressing sensitive issues. Having an objective third party can also help family members stay focused on solutions rather than getting lost in old patterns exacerbated by reactivity.

Finding Common Ground

Common ground often emerges in unexpected places. Sometimes it appears in shared memories of happier times, sometimes in mutual concern for future generations, and sometimes in the simple recognition of each other's humanity. The key is remaining open to discovering these connections even in the midst of disagreement.

The Treasure Beyond Conflict

Once again, imagine a family where members feel safe to express their needs and fears, where differences are met with curiosity instead of judgment, and where challenges become opportunities for growth. This isn't a utopian dream but a tangible reality for those willing to do the work.

The road to connection isn't easy, but it is worth it. As you embark on this journey, remember that you're not alone. There are tools, resources, and professionals ready to support you. And beyond the initial discomfort lies the treasure that makes it all worthwhile: the profound joy of knowing and being known, of loving and being loved.

Successful conflict resolution creates a foundation for effective mentoring and preparation of future generations, which we'll be exploring in the next chapter. When families can navigate disagreements skillfully, they're vastly better equipped to transfer both tangible and intangible wealth.

Closing Thoughts

Conflict is a natural part of life, but it need not define our relationships. By embracing it with an open heart and willingness to grow, we can transform it into a powerful force for connection and healing. The family treasure awaits those who dare to break the spell of conflict and embark on the path of reconciliation.

8

MENTORING AND PREPARATION

Nurturing the Next Generation's Growth

Imagine handing a teenager the keys to a Ferrari without any driver's training. The scenario sounds absurd, even dangerous. Yet many of us do something equally risky when we transfer wealth to the next generation without proper preparation. We hand over significant resources—whether financial assets, business responsibilities, or family legacies—to individuals who haven't been mentored in how to handle them wisely.

The Essential Need for Mentoring

Who among us doesn't need and long for mentoring and wisdom? Life grows more complex by the day. Whether we're learning to manage a budget, navigate relationships, or delve into an entirely new career, skill-building remains a lifelong process if we're honest with ourselves. The continual need for mentorship underscores our deep human desire for guidance, context, and nurturing as we grow.

One surefire way to harm our children's development—or maim the rising generation more broadly—is to skimp on or skip kind and patient mentorship. Consider Sarah, a young woman who inherited substantial wealth at twenty-one. Despite her intelligence and education, she found herself overwhelmed by the responsibility. "I felt like I was drowning," she told me. "Everyone assumed that because I had an economics degree, I would know how to handle this inheritance. But theory and reality are very different things."

Money only amplifies who we already are; it doesn't magically build character or equip us with the right habits. Like learning to drive, handling wealth responsibly requires practice, gentle correction, and an environment that both encourages curiosity and expects accountability.

Building on the foundation of safety we explored in Chapter 4, effective mentoring requires an environment where mistakes are viewed as learning opportunities rather than failures. The role flexibility discussed in Chapter 6 becomes especially important as mentors and mentees learn to shift between teaching and learning modes.

The Trust Fund Novice

Let's examine a concrete scenario: giving a trust fund to a 21-year-old who has no financial experience or context for the gift. Perhaps they've grown up in relative comfort, shielded from day-to-day concerns about budgeting, saving, or mindful spending. Suddenly, with a stroke of a pen, they gain access to substantial resources. Without the right understanding of how money works—or how emotions and human psychology influence spending and saving patterns—this young person may easily fall prey to reckless spending, misguided investments, or manipulative advisors.

James, a client whose story illustrates this point perfectly, inherited several million dollars on his twenty-first birthday. "Everyone thought I was set for life," he recalled. "Instead, I nearly destroyed myself. I had no framework for understanding what that money meant or how it could serve a larger purpose in my life." Within three years, James had burned through a third of his inheritance, strained relationships with family and friends, and developed anxiety about his ability to manage money responsibly.

Far from guaranteeing a secure future, an unearned windfall—absent mentorship—can lead to the dissolution of one's finances, relationships, and self-esteem. Many psychologists have documented a correlation between sudden wealth and self-destructive or externally manipulative behaviors, precisely because the individual has not developed the mental or emotional frameworks to navigate this newfound power.

The Difference Between Teaching and Mentoring

Mentoring differs fundamentally from traditional teaching in its emphasis on relationship, questioning, resourcefulness aspects, and shared experience. Jon Young's approach to "coyote mentoring" illustrates this beautifully. In coyote mentoring, the mentor doesn't simply provide answers; instead, they use leading questions that foster curiosity. A "coyote mentor" might notice a young person's interest in a certain topic, seize that moment of curiosity, and pose questions that challenge the mentee to think more deeply, to experiment, and to practice.

The essential elements of effective mentoring include:

- Building trust through consistent, supportive presence
- Asking questions that promote discovery rather than delivering answers
- Creating safe spaces for experimentation and failure
- Sharing personal experiences, including mistakes and lessons learned
- Celebrating growth and progress, no matter how small

These principles apply whether we're mentoring children about financial responsibility, preparing next-generation leaders for the family business, or helping young adults understand their role in family philanthropy.

The Emotional Core of Financial Decisions

Money is about far more than numbers. Research in behavioral finance repeatedly shows how emotions and cognitive biases influence our financial decisions and behavior. Hersh Shefrin points out that "people in standard finance are rational; people in behavioral finance are normal." Translated, this means that real human beings make decisions based on fear, greed, excitement, overconfidence, or social pressures—not purely on logic and available information.

Consider the case of the Martinez family. When the time came to transition their successful construction business to the next generation, they assumed their daughter Elena's MBA would prepare her for leadership. What they hadn't accounted for was the emotional weight of stepping into her father's shoes, managing longtime employees who still saw her as "little Elena," and dealing with her own perfectionist tendencies. Technical knowledge alone proved insufficient.

Through mentorship that addressed both practical and emotional aspects of leadership, Elena gradually developed confidence in her own style. Her father learned to step back gracefully, and together they created a transition plan that honored both innovation *and* tradition.

The Role of Values in Financial Mentoring

Money doesn't exist in a moral or psychological vacuum. We bring our hopes, fears, identities, and values to every financial decision we make. Parents and mentors who understand this integrate explicit values-based discussions into the learning journey.

The Harper family offers an illuminating example. Rather than simply giving their teenage children allowances, they created what they called "purpose accounts." Each child received funds divided into three categories: spending, saving, and giving. Regular family discussions explored not just the mechanics of managing these accounts but the deeper questions of value and purpose behind financial decisions.

Just as we saw in our discussion of family conflict (Chapter 7), alignment around core values provides a compass for navigating challenging conversations and decisions. The transparency principles from Chapter 5 become essential tools in the mentoring relationship.

Getting Young People "Invested"

The most successful mentoring occurs when young people feel genuinely invested—intellectually, emotionally, and sometimes financially—in their own learning process. Without personal investment, even the best advice tends to go unheeded. This requires connecting learning to goals or interests they already have, allowing them to experience real consequences (both positive and negative) on a manageable scale, and giving them meaningful autonomy in decision-making.

Critical factors for fostering investment include:

1. Personal relevance and meaning
2. Hands-on experience and practice
3. Graduated responsibility with appropriate support
4. Regular reflection and adjustment
5. Recognition of progress and achievement

The Power of Story: A Case Study in Successful Mentoring

Let me share the story of the Patel family, whose approach to mentoring transformed not just their children's financial acumen but their entire family culture. Instead of simply distributing inheritance or dictating rules about money, they created what they called their "Family Learning Laboratory."

Beginning when their children were young, they designated a portion of family funds for educational experiments. Each child could propose projects or investments they wanted to explore, with one crucial requirement: they had to research thoroughly and present their ideas to the family council. Some projects succeeded brilliantly; others failed instructively. But through this process, each child developed critical thinking skills, financial literacy, and the confidence to take calculated risks.

Today, the Patel children manage significant family assets while maintaining strong relationships with each other and their parents. Their story illustrates how thoughtful mentoring can nurture both financial competence and family cohesion.

Looking to the Future: Creating Regenerative Mentoring Systems

The most effective mentoring doesn't end with one generation teaching another. Instead, it creates what we might call "regenerative mentoring systems"—where those who have been mentored become skilled mentors themselves, perpetuating and evolving the family's wisdom.

This approach requires:

- Documenting lessons learned and best practices
- Creating opportunities for peer mentoring
- Maintaining flexibility to incorporate new ideas and approaches
- Building networks of support beyond the immediate family

When mentoring is grounded in the principles of safety, inclusion, and healthy conflict resolution we've explored throughout this book, it becomes a powerful vehicle for transmitting both tangible and intangible family wealth.

Conclusion: The Lifelong Journey of Learning and Teaching

Mentoring is not a one-time event but a continuous journey of mutual growth and discovery. When we approach it with patience, curiosity, and genuine care, we create lasting impact that extends far beyond financial success. We build emotional intelligence, strengthen family bonds, and nurture the human capacity for wisdom and generosity.

Investment in thoughtful mentoring pays dividends that no market return can beat: confident, capable individuals who understand both the privileges and responsibilities of wealth. More importantly, it creates families who know how to learn from each other, support each other's growth, and carry forward a legacy of wisdom that grows richer with each generation.

9

WELL BEING

The Source of True Wealth

The English language often holds subtle clues about human experience, and the origin of the word "wealth" offers a profound insight into what truly matters in life. Derived from the Old English word *weal*, meaning "well-being," wealth once meant far more than the mere accumulation of money or assets. It pointed to a way of life defined by vibrancy, contentment, social support, and holistic health—a state of flourishing that encompassed physical, emotional, social, and spiritual dimensions.

Reclaiming the Roots of Wealth

Sarah Chen sat in my office, outwardly the picture of success. Her family's investment firm had just completed its most profitable year yet. Her children attended prestigious schools, and her charitable foundation was making headlines for its innovative approach to education reform. Yet something was missing. "I have everything I'm supposed to want," she confided, "but I feel hollow inside. What's wrong with me?"

Nothing was wrong with Sarah. She had simply encountered the limitation of conventional wealth—the discovery that financial success alone cannot fulfill our deepest human needs. Her story reflects a broader truth: genuine prosperity springs from a more fundamental source than money. When we are healthy in mind and body, when our relationships are positive and supportive, and when our life purpose is clear, the fruits of what we traditionally call "wealth" begin to appear naturally.

The safety and trust we explored in Chapter 4 form the foundation for true well-being. Just as a garden needs secure boundaries to flourish, families need psychological safety to develop genuine prosperity.

The Foundation of Flourishing

Again, think of well-being like a garden. When a plant is placed in nutrient-rich soil, watered adequately, and exposed to the right amount of sunlight, it grows vigorously, produces beautiful blossoms, and bears fruit. Similarly, human beings whose physical, emotional, and social needs are met *tend to flourish*. Their energy levels rise, mental clarity improves, and confidence becomes more robust. Emotions remain generally positive, fueling creativity, resilience, and a collaborative spirit.

The Mason family learned this lesson through an unexpected crisis. When their third-generation manufacturing business faced a severe downturn, their initial response focused entirely on financial measures—cost-cutting, layoffs, and restructuring. But as family tensions mounted and decision-making became paralyzed by fear, their trusted advisor suggested a different approach. Instead of focusing solely on the balance sheet, they began attending to the family's collective well-being.

They instituted regular family meals where business talk was prohibited. They revived old traditions of weekend hiking trips. They created space for honest conversations about fears and hopes. Gradually, as their relationships strengthened and stress levels decreased, creative solutions to their business challenges emerged naturally. The company not only survived but transformed into a more resilient enterprise precisely because the family had invested in their fundamental well-being.

The inclusion principles we discussed in Chapter 5 become essential here - when all family members feel truly included, well-being naturally emerges. This connects directly to our exploration of breaking free from rigid roles (Chapter 6), as well-being requires the flexibility to grow beyond limiting labels.

The Science of Connection

Recent years have brought alarming research highlighting loneliness as one of the most significant threats to human health. Former U.S. Surgeon General Dr. Vivek Murthy has called loneliness an "epidemic" that shortens lifespans and undermines physical and mental well-being. His research shows that social isolation correlates with higher risks of heart disease, depression, and cognitive decline in older adults. Perhaps most sobering is the finding that loneliness increases the likelihood of early mortality by 26%—comparable to the risks associated with smoking.

These statistics take on special significance when we consider family wealth. The very pursuit of financial success can sometimes isolate us from the connections that sustain true well-being. Consider these *essential elements* of human connection:

- Safe and nurturing relationships
- Sense of belonging to a community
- Meaningful contribution to others
- Shared purpose and values
- Consistent emotional support

When these elements are present, families demonstrate remarkable resilience in facing challenges. When they're absent, no amount of financial wealth can compensate for the loss.

Remember our discussion of conflict in Chapter 7; even challenging moments can strengthen connection when handled with awareness. The mentoring practices we explored in Chapter 8 take on new meaning when viewed through the lens of well-being; they're not just about transferring knowledge but about nurturing whole-person development.

The Attributes of Connection

These attributes build upon all the principles we've explored so far:

- Safety and trust (Chapter 4) create the container
- Inclusion and transparency (Chapter 5) enable participation
- Role flexibility (Chapter 6) allows authentic expression
- Constructive conflict (Chapter 7) deepens understanding
- Mentoring relationships (Chapter 8) support growth

For more than four decades, educator and naturalist Jon Young has studied how connections—both to nature and to each other—transform communities and individuals. His research reveals a cluster of qualities that reliably emerge when people's "connection needs" are adequately fulfilled. These "Attributes of Connection" illuminate what becomes possible within a family deeply aligned in support, empathy, and shared growth.

The Rodriguez family exemplifies these attributes in action. Despite modest financial means, they maintained extraordinarily strong bonds across four generations. Their secret? Regular "council meetings" where every family member, from the youngest child to the eldest grandparent, had a voice. They practiced deep listening, celebrated each other's achievements (no matter how small), and faced challenges as a unified team. When unexpected wealth came into the family through the sale of their small business, these practiced connection skills helped ground them in navigating their new resources wisely.

Beyond Skepticism: The Power of Human Connection

For those who might doubt that these attributes spontaneously emerge from a well-connected life, the health data on loneliness offer a compelling counterargument. If isolation and emotional distance are so deadly that they top the list of major health risks, then strong connections—through familial bonds, friendships, community involvement, or spiritual fellowship—may represent the most vital life-protecting and life-enhancing condition available to us.

The Bennett family discovered this truth through tragedy. After losing their patriarch to suicide—a successful businessman who had everything except close relationships—they committed to transforming their family culture. They began prioritizing emotional check-ins over financial updates. They invested in family therapy and communication training. Most importantly, they started seeing each other as human beings first, role-players in a family system second.

Morality from the Inside Out

One of the most surprising *outcomes* of having our connection needs met is the development of an internal moral compass. Darcia Narvaez, in her groundbreaking book "Neurobiology and the Development of Human Morality," demonstrates that morality emerges from the inside out, guided by empathy, emotional attunement, and a sense of secure belonging. When individuals experience deep connection, they become less reliant on external rules and more guided by internal values and concern for others.

This has profound implications for family wealth and legacy planning. Instead of focusing solely on controlling behavior through trust provisions or inheritance conditions, families might better serve their long-term interests by investing in the conditions that naturally foster ethical behavior and wise decision-making.

The Collective Price of Disconnection

Understanding the value of connection begs the question: Why do so many societies struggle with widespread disconnection? Modern life often works against our innate need for connection. Many people commute long distances alone, work in isolating environments, and rarely engage face-to-face in community activities. Educational systems frequently neglect social-emotional learning in favor of standardized testing, while demanding work schedules leave little energy for cultivating relationships.

The consequences appear in high rates of depression, anxiety, substance abuse, and physical illness. When needs for belonging, affection, and meaning go unmet, humans seek substitutes—ranging from unhealthy habits to addictive behaviors. Communities weakened by disconnection become vulnerable to harmful ideologies that thrive on fear and alienation.

Cultivating Well-Being in Family Systems

Families serve as the fundamental building blocks of human society, where individuals ideally first learn to give and receive love, resolve conflict, and care for one another. When families prioritize well-being through intentional self-care and nurturing of relationships, everyone benefits. The synergy of connection flows in multiple directions: parents support children, children invigorate parents, extended relatives contribute wisdom and resources, and the broader community is enriched by stable, thriving families.

Notice how the practices we're discussing integrate earlier themes:

- Safe spaces for vulnerability (Chapter 4)
- Inclusive decision-making (Chapter 5)
- Freedom from rigid roles (Chapter 6)
- Healthy conflict navigation (Chapter 7)
- Cross-generational learning (Chapter 8)

The Path Forward

Creating a culture of well-being within families requires conscious effort and regular attention. Just as a garden needs consistent tending, family well-being needs ongoing cultivation. Here are key practices that support this cultivation:

1. Regular family gatherings focused on connection rather than business
2. Shared activities that promote joy and play
3. Open communication about emotions and needs
4. Recognition and celebration of individual and collective achievements
5. Support for personal growth and development

Conclusion: Well-Being as the True Family Treasure

Revisiting the original meaning of *"wealth"* as *well-being* reminds us that the state of thriving isn't a utopian dream but a tangible reality waiting to be activated. It requires intentional self-care, relational nurturing, and grounding in the larger networks of community and nature. When these elements align, the family ecosystem comes alive, producing a veritable treasure of "fruits": supportive relationships, creative resourcefulness, resilience, moral clarity, and profound peace.

In a world of rapid technological change and mounting societal pressures, the power of genuine human connection stands as both anchor and beacon. It calls us to remember that no individual is an island, and that our shared humanity represents both our greatest vulnerability and our greatest strength. As we cultivate well-being in ourselves, we uplift those around us, contributing to a regenerative cycle of empathy, trust, and innovation. This renewed sense of "wealth" might just be the most crucial inheritance we can offer our children and our communities.

Well-being represents the culmination of all we've discussed—it's what becomes possible when families create safety, practice inclusion, transcend limiting roles, navigate conflict skillfully, and support each other's growth through mentoring.

10

REGENERATIVE FAMILY DYNAMICS

Creating a Vibrant Family Legacy

Picture two ancient redwood trees standing side by side in a forest. One has grown straight and tall, its branches reaching skyward, while the other has grown twisted, adapting to storms and obstacles in its path. Both trees are equally majestic, equally alive, and equally important to the forest ecosystem. Similarly, families that thrive across generations don't simply maintain a rigid status quo—they adapt, evolve, and often grow stronger through life's challenges.

Beyond Resilience

When we talk about "Regenerative Family Dynamics," we're stepping beyond simple resilience. While "resilience" suggests returning to a previous steady state after disruption, "regenerative" implies improvement, evolution, and flourishing in the face of challenges. The Thompson family's story illustrates this distinction perfectly.

After losing their family business to a devastating fire, the Thompsons could have focused solely on rebuilding what was lost. Instead, they used this crisis as an opportunity to reimagine their entire enterprise. They gathered their children and grandchildren, not just to reconstruct the business, but to envision how it could better serve their values and community. The result? A more innovative company, stronger family bonds, and a deeper sense of purpose that engaged the next generation.

Regenerative families don't just bounce back after difficulties—they grow stronger, adapt creatively, and harness new opportunities, often turning adversity into a catalyst for transformation.

Core Values as Bedrock

Values serve as both operating principles and aspirations in regenerative families. The Martinez family demonstrates how values create continuity through change. For three generations, they've maintained a successful real estate development company. But what truly sets them apart isn't their business acumen—it's their commitment to core values that guide every decision:

Essential Family Values:

- Respect and dignity for all
- Honesty and transparency
- Stewardship and sustainability
- Innovation balanced with tradition
- Service to community
- Growth and lifelong learning

These aren't just words on a family charter. When the youngest generation proposed shifting their developments toward affordable housing and environmental sustainability, the family used these values as a framework for discussion. Instead of dismissing the idea as too risky or unconventional, they explored how it aligned with their commitment to community service and stewardship.

Adaptability and Continuous Learning

The Chan family's journey exemplifies how regenerative dynamics foster adaptation. As their traditional import-export business faced disruption from digital commerce and tariffs, they didn't merely try to protect their existing model. Instead, they created what they called "learning laboratories" where family members could experiment with new approaches.

Their quarterly family meetings transformed from status updates to interactive workshops. Younger members shared insights about emerging technologies while older generations contributed wisdom about relationship-building and negotiation. Their willingness to learn from each other enabled them to pivot successfully into e-commerce services while maintaining the relationship-centered approach that had always been their strength.

Creativity and Innovation

Regenerative families intentionally create safe spaces for experimentation. The Patel family exemplifies this approach through their "Family Innovation Fund." Each year, they allocate resources for family members to propose and test new business ideas or philanthropic initiatives. Their only requirements? Projects must align with family values and include multiple generations in their execution.

Some ventures succeed brilliantly; others fail instructively. But through this process, family members develop entrepreneurial skills, learn to collaborate across generations, and maintain the creative spark that prevents stagnation.

Recall our discussion of inclusion and transparency in Chapter 5. The Patel family's 'Family Innovation Fund' works precisely because it incorporates those principles of open communication and collaborative decision-making.

Strengthening the Human Side

While technical aspects of estate planning—like wills, trusts, and tax strategies—matter deeply, regenerative families recognize that human elements form the foundation of lasting success. The Rodriguez family demonstrates this principle through their approach to succession planning.

Instead of focusing solely on transferring business responsibilities, they invested in building emotional intelligence and relationship skills. Monthly family councils provide space for open dialogue about hopes, fears, and dreams. Younger members receive mentoring not just in business operations but in understanding family dynamics, managing relationships, and the stewardship of limited resources.

Key elements of their human-centered approach include:

1. Structured communication forums
2. Cross-generational mentoring programs
3. Emotional intelligence development
4. Conflict resolution training
5. Regular celebration of relationships

The conflict resolution tools from Chapter 7 and the mentoring approaches from Chapter 8 provide practical ways to nurture the human elements of regenerative systems. When families can navigate disagreements skillfully and support intergenerational learning, they create conditions for continuous renewal.

The well-being principles we explored in Chapter 9 form the foundation for regenerative leadership. When families prioritize holistic health - physical, emotional, relational, and spiritual - they create the conditions for sustainable growth and innovation.

The Legacy of Leadership

Consider the Williams family, who transformed their approach to leadership after nearly losing their business to internal conflict. Rather than maintaining centralized control, they developed what they call "distributed wisdom"—a system where different family members lead in areas of their strength while remaining accountable to shared values.

Their family meetings now rotate leadership roles, allowing each member to develop facilitation skills. Decision-making involves genuine collaboration rather than top-down directives. Most importantly, they've learned to value diverse perspectives as a source of innovation rather than seeing differences as threats to unity.

Why "Regenerative" Matters Today

The pace of change—economically, technologically, and environmentally—demands that families develop regenerative capabilities. The Kumar family discovered this truth when their traditional manufacturing business faced disruption from artificial intelligence and automation. Instead of resisting change, they embraced it as an opportunity for regeneration.

They engaged every generation in exploring how technology could enhance rather than replace their human-centered approach to business. Younger family members led digital transformation initiatives while older generations ensured that technological changes aligned with their values of craftsmanship and employee care. Their willingness to evolve while maintaining core principles enabled them to thrive in changing conditions.

Creating Regenerative Systems

The Greene family's approach to family governance illustrates how regenerative dynamics work in practice. Rather than establishing rigid rules, they created what they call "learning frameworks"—flexible structures that encourage growth while maintaining necessary boundaries.

Their family constitution includes regular review and amendment processes. Their investment committee intentionally combines experienced members with younger voices. Even their philanthropic activities involve continuous learning, with each generation encouraged to explore new approaches to creating social impact.

Looking Forward

Regenerative Family Dynamics represents more than a theoretical framework—it offers practical tools for creating lasting impact across generations. When families embrace regenerative principles, they develop:

- Greater adaptability to change
- Stronger cross-generational bonds
- Enhanced problem-solving capabilities
- Deeper alignment with values
- Sustained creativity and innovation

Conclusion

- The future belongs to families who can grow, adapt, and evolve while maintaining their essential values and connections. Like those ancient redwoods in the forest, regenerative families will face storms and challenges, but they grow stronger through adversity, supporting each other while reaching ever higher.

- The regenerative approach builds upon all we've explored: the safety principles of Chapter 4, the inclusion practices of Chapter 5, the role flexibility of Chapter 6, the constructive conflict of Chapter 7, the mentoring wisdom of Chapter 8, and the well-being focus of Chapter 9.

- By embedding regenerative principles into their culture, governance, and planning, families create something far more valuable than mere wealth—they nurture an evolving legacy that can truly serve and inspire future generations. In this way, family resources become not just assets to preserve but catalysts for continuous growth and positive impact in an ever-changing world.

A regenerative family system integrates all the elements we've explored throughout this book:

- Safety and trust enable risk-taking and innovation
- Inclusion ensures all voices contribute to growth
- Flexible roles allow adaptation to change
- Constructive conflict drives evolution
- Mentoring supports continuous learning
- Well-being provides sustainable energy for growth

PART III
PUTTING IT ALL TOGETHER

11

PUTTING IT ALL TOGETHER

Integrating the Elements of Lasting Family Success

Maria Santiago stood at the window of her family's beach house, watching the sunset paint the sky in brilliant oranges and pinks. Behind her, the sounds of laughter and conversation drifted from the dining room where three generations of her family gathered for their monthly dinner. Two years ago, such a peaceful scene would have seemed impossible. The family business had been in crisis, siblings weren't speaking to each other, and their parents' estate plan had become a source of bitter conflict.

What changed? How did the Santiagos transform from a family in crisis to one that now serves as a model of multigenerational harmony? Their journey illustrates how the principles we've explored throughout this book can work together to create lasting positive change.

The Journey So Far

Over the course of this book, we've explored how thoughtful, intentional family conversations around legacy planning can lead to far richer outcomes than most people imagine. We began by examining why families often avoid these crucial conversations, which can include a fear of conflict, anxiety over hurting each other's feelings, and/or uncertainty about where to even begin. We discovered that successful estate planning and family communication are inextricably linked, and that focusing solely on technical or legal aspects neglects the human components that can either bring families closer together or drive them apart.

The Santiago family's transformation began when they realized that their challenges weren't primarily technical or legal—though those elements needed attention—but rather centered on human dynamics and communication patterns that had developed over decades.

Building on Strong Foundations

The family's first step involved creating psychological safety—that essential condition we explored in Chapter 4. They worked with a skilled facilitator who helped them establish basic ground rules for communication:

- Listen to understand, not to respond
- Speak from personal experience rather than accusation
- Honor confidentiality within the family
- Acknowledge emotions without letting them control discussions
- Focus on solutions while learning from the past

With these foundations in place, family members gradually began sharing thoughts and feelings they'd previously kept hidden. Maria's brother Robert revealed his fear that his creative approach to business would never be valued. Their sister Elena expressed her concern about being excluded from key decisions despite her financial expertise. Their parents shared their worry about being seen as controlling when they were actually more interested in protecting family harmony.

The Power of Inclusion

Following the principles outlined in Chapter 5, the Santiagos made inclusion and transparency central to their family culture. They created regular forums for sharing information and making decisions collectively. Monthly family dinners became more than social gatherings—though maintaining that social connection remained crucial. They developed a rhythm of alternating between purely social time and structured discussions about family business, philanthropy, and legacy planning.

Key elements that supported their success included integration practices, such as:

- Regular family meetings with clear agendas
- Rotating leadership roles to develop new skills
- Mentoring partnerships across generations
- Open access to relevant financial information
- Clear processes for raising concerns and suggestions

Breaking Free from Old Roles

The insights about family roles from Chapter 6 proved particularly valuable for the Santiagos. They began recognizing how locked-in role assignments had limited their growth and adaptability. Robert wasn't just "the creative one," Elena wasn't just "the responsible one," and their parents weren't just "the decision makers." By consciously expanding beyond these confining labels, each family member discovered new capabilities and ways to contribute.

Finding Common Ground

The Collaborative Practice principles discussed in Chapter 7 helped the family navigate their differences more effectively. Instead of viewing conflicts as threats to harmony, they learned to see them as opportunities for deeper understanding and creative problem-solving. When disagreements arose about the direction of the family business, they used structured dialogue techniques to explore underlying interests rather than becoming entrenched in positions.

Preparing the Next Generation

Building on the mentoring principles from Chapter 8, the Santiagos developed a comprehensive approach to preparing future generations for their roles in the family enterprise. Rather than simply hoping young family members would figure things out, they created intentional learning experiences that combined practical skills with emotional intelligence development.

They established what they called "learning laboratories" where younger family members could experiment with leadership and decision-making in low-risk settings. The family's philanthropic foundation proved particularly valuable for this purpose, allowing next-generation members to develop grant-making strategies and evaluate social impact while being mentored by more experienced family members.

Nurturing Well-Being

The emphasis on well-being discussed in Chapter 9 transformed how the Santiagos viewed success. They began measuring their prosperity not just by financial metrics but by the quality of their relationships, the vitality of their connections, and their impact on the broader community. Regular check-ins about emotional and spiritual well-being became as important as financial updates.

Embracing Regenerative Dynamics

The principles of Regenerative Family Dynamics from Chapter 10 helped the Santiagos create systems that could evolve and grow stronger over time. They learned to see change not as a threat to tradition but as an opportunity for renewal and innovation. Their governance structures became more flexible, allowing for adaptation while maintaining alignment with core values.

The Path Forward

The Santiago family's journey illustrates how the various elements we've explored work together synergistically. Each principle reinforces the others, creating a robust framework for family flourishing. However, their story also demonstrates that transformation doesn't happen overnight. It requires patience, commitment, and willingness to learn from setbacks.

Practical Implementation

For families beginning this journey, consider starting with these foundational steps:

1. Create safe spaces for open dialogue
2. Establish regular family meetings
3. Develop clear communication protocols
4. Invest in relationship building
5. Focus on preparing future generations
6. Maintain flexibility in structures and processes

7. Regularly review and adjust approaches

The Human Element

Throughout their journey, the Santiagos discovered that technical excellence in estate planning, while important, matters far less than the human elements of trust, understanding, and shared purpose. They learned to see their family as a living system that requires constant nurturing rather than a mechanical structure that can be set once and forgotten.

Looking Ahead

As we move into our final chapter, we'll explore how to craft your family's unique recipe for legacy success. Using the metaphor of cooking and baking, we'll examine how to combine essential technical ingredients with crucial human elements, understand proper timing and preparation, and create a legacy plan that's uniquely suited to your family.

Remember: Just as every celebrated chef began with simple dishes, your family's journey toward excellence starts with basic steps. The Santiago family's transformation didn't happen overnight, but rather through consistent, intentional effort. As we move into our final chapter, you'll learn:

- How to identify and combine essential technical and human ingredients
- The importance of proper preparation and timing

- Ways to test and adjust your approach
- The role of experienced guidance in the process
- How to create and maintain your family's unique legacy recipe

Let's turn now to 'The Perfect Recipe,' where we'll translate everything we've explored into a framework for creating your family's unique approach to lasting success.

12

THE PERFECT RECIPE

Crafting Your Family's Unique Legacy Plan

In my grandmother's kitchen hung a worn, yellow recipe card for her famous apple pie. The card listed ingredients and basic steps, but ask any family member who tried to recreate her masterpiece—something was always missing. The secret, we eventually learned, wasn't in the ingredients themselves but in how she combined them, the way she knew exactly when to adjust the spices, how she could tell by touch when the dough was just right. Her pie wasn't just about following instructions; it was about understanding the art of bringing elements together to create something greater than the sum of its parts.

Legacy planning bears a striking resemblance to my grandmother's approach to baking. While can list the essential ingredients—legal documents, family meetings, communication protocols—the magic lies in how we combine and adjust these elements to suit each family's unique flavor and circumstances.

The Essential Ingredients

Every masterful recipe begins with quality ingredients. For legacy planning, these fundamentals include:

- A well-drafted will
- Advanced healthcare directives
- Powers of attorney
- Trust documents (when appropriate)
- Asset inventory
- Digital asset management
- End-of-life instructions

However, just as a list of ingredients doesn't make a pie, these documents alone don't create a lasting legacy. The Martinez family learned this lesson when their meticulously crafted estate plan nearly tore them apart. Despite having every legal document perfectly prepared, they had neglected the human elements that make a legacy plan work.

Adding the Human Elements

Just as my grandmother knew that the feeling of the dough mattered more than exact measurements, successful families recognize that the intangible elements often matter most. The

Patel family exemplifies this understanding. Beyond their formal estate plan, they weave in essential human ingredients:

- Regular family storytelling sessions
- Cross-generational mentoring
- Shared philanthropic projects
- Cultural tradition celebrations
- Personal legacy letters to future generations

These human elements transform their legacy plan from a mere set of instructions into a living, breathing expression of family values.

The Art of Preparation

Consider the story of the Kim family, whose approach to legacy planning transformed after their patriarch's health scare. Rather than rushing to update documents in crisis, they began what they called their "Legacy Kitchen"—regular gatherings where family members could practice working together, share stories, and gradually develop the skills needed for successful wealth transition.

Like master chefs practicing mise en place—getting everything in order before beginning—they:

- Assembled their team of advisors (legal, financial, family dynamics)
- Gathered important documents
- Created secure systems for sharing information

- Established regular meeting schedules
- Developed communication protocols

Testing and Adjusting

No chef creates the perfect recipe on the first try. The Reynolds family demonstrates how iteration and adjustment strengthen legacy plans. They treat their quarterly family meetings like test kitchens, experimenting with different approaches to decision-making and communication. When something doesn't work, they adjust the recipe rather than abandoning the whole effort.

During one particularly challenging discussion about their family business succession, they discovered that breaking the conversation into smaller, more focused sessions—like dividing a complex recipe into manageable steps—allowed for better understanding and participation from all family members.

Timing Matters

Like any complex dish, legacy planning requires attention to timing. The Chen family learned this when they tried to rush their succession planning. Just as you can't speed up the proper baking of a soufflé, you can't rush the development of trust and understanding in a family.

They adjusted their approach to recognize that different elements need different timing:

- Some ingredients need to marinate (building trust)
- Others require slow simmering (developing shared values)
- A few elements must be added at precisely the right moment (key decisions)
- Certain aspects need time to rest (processing emotional changes)
- Many components improve with age (deepening relationships)

The Role of the Master Chef

Every great kitchen benefits from experienced leadership. In family legacy planning, this often means working with skilled advisors who, like master chefs, understand both technique and timing. The Thompson family found their turning point when they engaged a family enterprise consultant who, like a master chef teaching advanced techniques, helped them understand the principles behind successful wealth transition rather than just following a rigid recipe.

These "master chefs" help families:

- Understand the science behind the art
- Recognize when adjustments are needed
- Maintain the right temperature (emotional climate)
- Balance different flavors (perspectives)
- Know when to stir things up and when to let them settle

When Things Don't Turn Out as Expected

Even the best chefs occasionally burn a dish. The Rodriguez family's story offers valuable lessons in recovery after their first attempt at succession planning failed. Instead of giving up, they:

- Analyzed what went wrong
- Adjusted their approach
- Strengthened family communication
- Built in more feedback loops
- Celebrated small improvements

Creating Your Own Recipe

While this book offers frameworks and guidelines, each family must ultimately create its own unique recipe for success. The Goldstein family's approach illustrates this beautifully. They took basic estate planning ingredients but added their own special elements:

- Monthly cooking lessons that combined family business discussions with actual meal preparation
- Story cards that captured family wisdom alongside favorite recipes
- Investment decisions made while sharing traditional family meals
- Philanthropy projects that included feeding the community

Looking to the Future

Like any great recipe, a family legacy plan should be both preservable and adaptable. The best family recipes evolve while maintaining their essential character—just as the best legacy plans allow for growth and change while preserving core values.

The Joy in the Journey

Remember that like cooking, legacy planning should involve joy and creativity alongside its more serious aspects. The most successful families find ways to make the process engaging and meaningful for all generations. They understand that the time spent in the kitchen together—planning, preparing, and sharing—often matters more than the final dish itself.

Conclusion: Your Family's Signature Dish

In the end, your family's legacy plan should be like a beloved family recipe—unique to your family yet built on time-tested principles. It should reflect your values, accommodate individual tastes, and create something that nourishes future generations.

As you move forward with your own legacy planning, remember my grandmother's apple pie. The recipe card provided a foundation, but the magic emerged from understanding, experience, and love. Your family's legacy plan needs both structure and heart, technique and intuition, tradition and innovation.

May your efforts create a legacy that, like the aroma of fresh-baked pie, draws family together and creates memories that span generations.

*Pay attention to what you're longing for.
Others may be longing for it, too.*

— Jon Young

Appendices

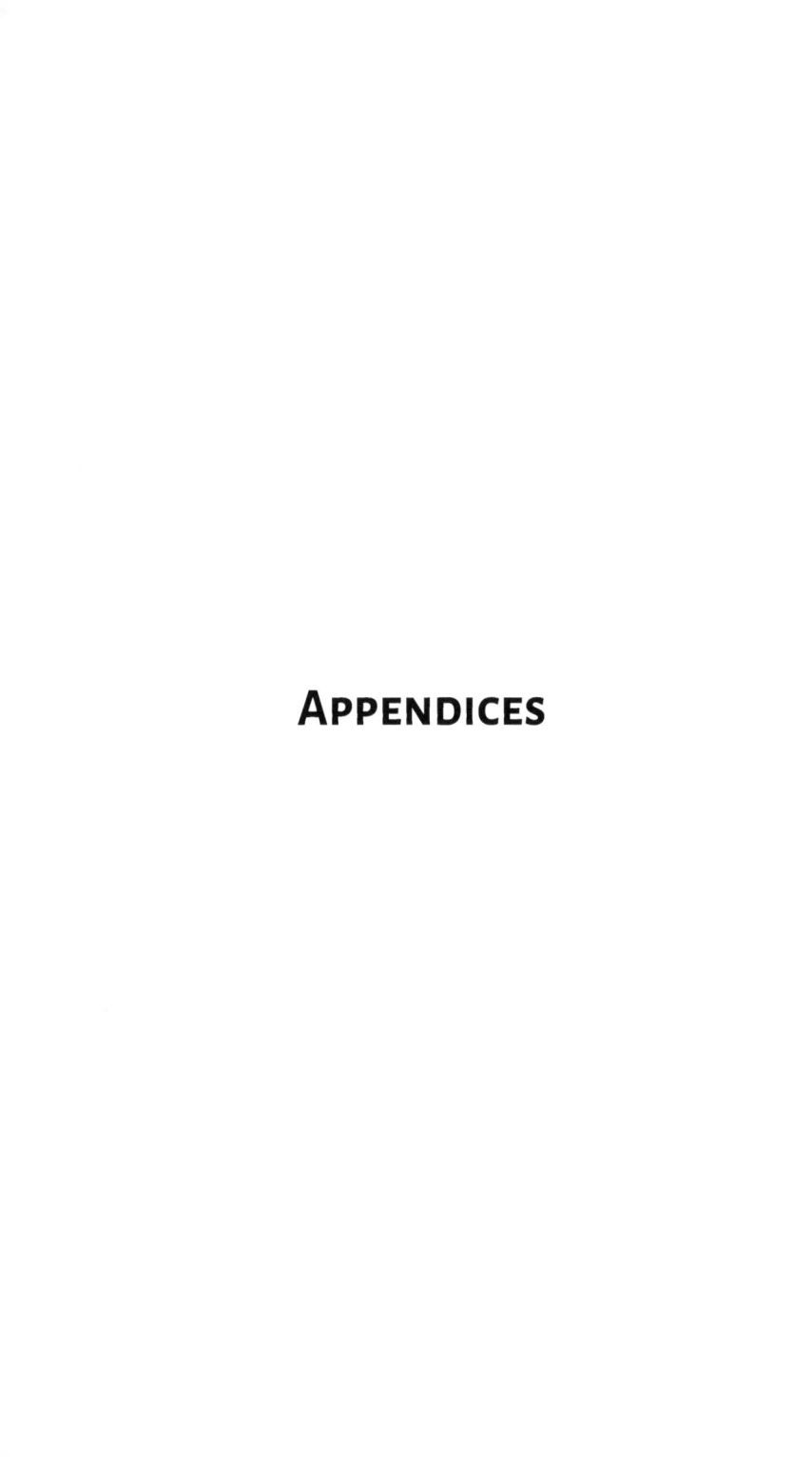

APPENDIX I

Willing Wisdom Index: An Innovative Online Estate Planning Tool

Overview

The Willing Wisdom Index is a groundbreaking online tool designed to help individuals and families take the first critical steps toward creating a meaningful estate plan. Unlike traditional estate planning, which often focuses solely on legal documents, the Willing Wisdom Index emphasizes personal values, family communication, and legacy-building.

The Offer

Our firm, PWJohnson Wealth & Legacy, LLC, maintains an institutional user license for the Willing Wisdom Index, and we make it available as a public service for clients and the public. You have free access to this $199 evaluation, which you can use to gauge your estate planning readiness and get a clear picture of next steps tailored to your needs. No one — not even our firm — can see your Index scores or information, unless you choose to share it.

To access The Willing Wisdom Index at no cost or obligation, simply use this link:

tinyurl.com/WillingWisdomIndex

Key Features & Benefits

- Comprehensive Self-Assessment – Users answer a series of thought-provoking questions to evaluate their preparedness for estate planning, identifying gaps in their current approach.

- Personalized Report – Upon completion, users receive a customized report with actionable insights to enhance their estate planning process.

- Family Communication Focus – Encourages open and honest discussions among loved ones about wealth, values, and the intentions behind estate decisions.

- Guidance Without Complexity – Provides clear, easy-to-understand recommendations without requiring immediate legal or financial expertise.

- Privacy & Security – Ensures that personal responses remain confidential while delivering insights that can be shared with advisors and family members.

- Integration with Professional Advice – Complements traditional estate planning by helping individuals approach their financial and legal advisors with clarity and purpose.

Why It Matters

Estate planning is about more than just distributing assets—it's about ensuring your wishes are honored, minimizing family conflict, and leaving a lasting legacy. The Willing Wisdom Index empowers individuals to take a proactive, thoughtful approach to estate planning while strengthening family relationships and fostering open dialogue.

Using the Willing Wisdom Index, individuals can make informed decisions that align with their values, ensuring their estate plan reflects not just what they own, but who they are and what they care about most.

APPENDIX II

Resources for Learning About the Basics of Estate Planning

Books

1. "Estate Planning for Dummies" – *N. Brian Caverly & Jordan S. Simon. A beginner-friendly guide covering wills, trusts, and tax implications.*
2. "Beyond the Grave: The Right Way and the Wrong Way of Leaving Money to Your Children" – *Jeffrey Condon. Addresses common mistakes families make in estate planning.*
3. "The Complete Book of Wills, Estates, & Trusts" – *Alexander A. Bove Jr. A thorough and practical guide for estate planning essentials.*
4. "Plan Your Estate" – *Denis Clifford. A plain-English guide to estate planning, probate, and asset protection.*
5. "The Family Estate Planning Guide" – *Trusts & Estates Magazine. Great for high-net-worth individuals looking for advanced strategies.*

Websites & Online Guides

1. Nolo.com – www.nolo.com *Provides easy-to-understand legal articles and estate planning forms.*
2. WealthCounsel – www.wealthcounsel.com. *Geared toward estate planning professionals but useful for clients as well.*
3. American Bar Association (ABA) Estate Planning FAQ – www.americanbar.org. *Covers fundamental estate planning topics and legal considerations.*
4. Investopedia: Estate Planning Guide – www.investopedia.com. *Explains key terms, strategies, and planning tools.*
5. CFPB Guide to Estate Planning – www.consumerfinance.gov *Great for elder financial planning and estate basics.*

Estate Planning Tools & Calculators

1. Estate Planning Questionnaire (PDF Download) – Many estate planning attorneys provide checklists. You can create one or find a generic version online.
2. Intuit's Estate Tax Calculator – Helps estimate estate tax liability.
3. Everplans – www.everplans.com. *A digital vault for estate planning documents, passwords, and important files.*
4. Legacy Shield – A secure document storage and estate planning service.

Videos & Podcasts

1. YouTube: "Estate Planning Basics" by Khan Academy – Explains wills, trusts, and probate.
2. TED Talk: "Why You Should Have a Will" by David R. Dow – A compelling look at why planning matters.
3. Podcast: "Smart Passive Income – Estate Planning Episode" – A business-minded approach to estate planning.
4. Podcast: "The Retirement and IRA Show" – Covers tax and estate planning strategies.

State-Specific Resources

1. FindLaw State Probate Laws – www.findlaw.com. *Helps clients understand local estate planning laws.*
2. Local Bar Association Websites – Many state bar associations provide estate planning guides.

APPENDIX III

How to Select an Estate Planning Attorney

Estate planning attorneys specialize in helping individuals and families organize their assets, plan for incapacity, and ensure their wishes are carried out after death. They provide legal guidance on wills, trusts, tax strategies, powers of attorney, and healthcare directives. A well-drafted estate plan minimizes legal complications, protects beneficiaries, and can reduce taxes and probate costs.

What an Estate Planning Attorney Does

- Drafts Essential Documents: Prepares wills, trusts, and advance healthcare directives to ensure assets are distributed according to your wishes.
- Minimizes Taxes and Costs: Helps structure your estate to reduce estate taxes and avoid unnecessary probate expenses.

- Plans for Incapacity: Establishes durable powers of attorney and healthcare directives so trusted individuals can make decisions if you become unable to.
- Protects Beneficiaries: Creates trusts to safeguard inheritances, especially for minor children, individuals with special needs, or those prone to financial mismanagement.
- Avoids Probate Complications: Helps set up estate plans that streamline or bypass the probate process, ensuring faster and smoother asset transfers.
- Advises on Complex Estates: Provides legal strategies for business owners, blended families, and individuals with significant or unique assets.

How to Select an Estate Planning Attorney

1. Look for Specialization – Choose an attorney with expertise in estate planning, trust law, and probate, rather than a general practitioner.
2. Check Credentials – Look for certifications such as Certified Specialist in Estate Planning, Trust & Probate Law (in applicable states). Membership in organizations like the American College of Trust and Estate Counsel (ACTEC) is a plus.
3. Assess Experience – An experienced attorney will be well-versed in handling estates similar to yours, including tax planning, charitable giving, and business succession.

4. Ask About Their Process – A good estate planner will take time to understand your situation, educate you on your options, and provide clear guidance.
5. Discuss Fees Upfront – Estate planning attorneys charge flat fees for many services, but some may bill hourly. Ensure you understand their pricing structure.
6. Read Client Reviews – Online testimonials, referrals from financial advisors, or recommendations from friends and family can help identify a trustworthy attorney.
7. Ensure Comfort and Communication – You should feel comfortable discussing personal and financial matters with your attorney, and they should be responsive to your needs.

Conclusion

A well-qualified estate planning attorney provides more than just legal documents—they create a strategy to protect your wealth, family, and legacy. By carefully selecting an attorney with the right expertise, experience, and approach, you can ensure peace of mind for yourself and your loved ones.

APPENDIX IV

Recommended Reading List

- *The Last Things We Talk About*, Elizabeth Boatwright, PhD
  The *Last Things We Talk About* is a compassionate and practical guide to navigating the difficult conversations surrounding death and end-of-life planning. Written by Elizabeth Boatwright, a hospice chaplain and certified financial planner, the book provides insights into the emotional, financial, and medical aspects of preparing for the inevitable. It blends real-life stories with actionable advice, helping individuals and families face mortality with greater peace and preparedness.

  https://www.amazon.com/dp/978-1945188350

- *Hug of War*, Cathy Carroll
  Hug of War explores the intricate dynamics of family businesses, offering guidance on how to navigate conflicts, maintain relationships, and ensure business

continuity. Cathy Carroll, an experienced family business consultant, provides a deeply insightful look into the struggles and triumphs of families working together, blending personal stories with practical wisdom. The book is a must-read for anyone seeking to strengthen both family bonds and business success.

https://www.amazon.com/dp/979-8888243640

- *Willing Wisdom*, Tom Deans, PhD
  Willing Wisdom challenges conventional estate planning by emphasizing the importance of open, honest conversations about wealth and legacy. Tom Deans, PhD, argues that the best estate plans are built on transparency and shared values, rather than secrecy and rigid legal documents. Through engaging storytelling and thought-provoking questions, the book encourages families to approach inheritance planning as an opportunity for meaningful connection rather than conflict.

  https://www.amazon.com/dp/978-0980891027

- *Othering and Belonging*, John A Powell
  Othering and Belonging is a profound exploration of the social forces that divide and unite us, written by renowned scholar John A. Powell. The book examines the mechanisms of exclusion—such as racism, inequality, and polarization—while offering strategies

for fostering inclusive communities where everyone feels a sense of belonging. Grounded in research and real-world examples, it provides a roadmap for building a more just and interconnected society.

https://www.amazon.com/dp/978-1503638846

- *The Gift of Lift*, David R. York
  The Gift of Lift redefines legacy, arguing that true wealth isn't just about financial inheritance but about lifting others up through generosity, mentorship, and shared purpose. David R. York, an estate planning attorney, explores the impact of intentional giving and how individuals can create a lasting, positive influence on their families and communities. The book offers a fresh, inspiring perspective on how to leave a meaningful legacy beyond material assets.

  https://www.amazon.com/dp/978-1646636617

APPENDIX V

Online Services

1. Quicken WillMaker & Trust by Nolo
   https://www.nolo.com/products/quicken-willmaker-trust.
   Quicken WillMaker & Trust is a comprehensive estate planning software that guides users through creating wills, trusts, and other essential documents. It offers a user-friendly interface and state-specific legal forms, making it accessible for individuals seeking to manage their estate planning needs independently.

2. Trust & Will
   https://trustandwill.com
   Trust & Will provides an intuitive platform for creating customized estate planning documents, including wills, trusts, and guardianships. With state-specific templates and a straightforward process, users can complete their estate plans efficiently.

3. LegalZoom
   https://www.legalzoom.com
   LegalZoom offers a range of legal services, including estate planning. Users can create wills, living trusts, and powers of attorney with guidance from legal professionals. The platform also provides access to attorney consultations for personalized assistance.

4. Rocket Lawyer
   https://www.rocketlawyer.com
   Rocket Lawyer provides online legal services, including estate planning documents like wills and trusts. The platform offers a free trial and membership options that include access to legal advice and document reviews by attorneys.

5. GoodTrust
   https://www.mygoodtrust.com
   GoodTrust specializes in digital estate planning, allowing users to manage both traditional and digital assets. The platform offers tools to create wills, trusts, and directives, as well as a digital vault for storing important documents and account information.

6. Do Your Own Will?
   https://www.doyourownwill.com
   Your Own Will offers free templates for creating wills, living wills, and power of attorney documents. The

platform is straightforward and suitable for individuals seeking basic estate planning solutions without incurring costs.

7. Fabric by Gerber Life
   https://meetfabric.com
   Fabric provides free online will creation services tailored for young families. The platform simplifies the process of appointing guardians and beneficiaries, making it accessible for those new to estate planning.

8. LawDepot
   https://www.lawdepot.com
   LawDepot offers a wide range of legal document templates, including those for estate planning such as wills, trusts, and powers of attorney. Users can customize documents to fit their specific needs and access them through various subscription options.

9. Everplans
   https://www.everplans.com
   Everplans is a digital platform that helps users organize and securely store important documents, account information, and end-of-life wishes. It serves as a comprehensive resource for estate planning and legacy management, ensuring that loved ones have access to vital information when needed

10. Vanilla

    https://www.justvanilla.com

    Vanilla offers tools for financial advisors and clients to streamline the estate planning process. The platform provides resources and guidance to help users understand and implement essential estate planning strategies effectively.

Made in the USA
Columbia, SC
22 April 2025